THE WOMEN WHO REVOLUTIONIZED FASHION

THE WON

REVOLUT

250 YEARS OF DESIGN

EDITED BY PETRA SLINKARD WITH CONTRIBUTIONS BY MADELIEF HOHÉ, LAN MORGAN, PAULA B. RICHTER, PETRA SLINKARD, AND RACHEL SYME

PEABODY ESSEX MUSEUM SALEM, MASSACHUSETTS   IN COLLABORATION WITH KUNSTMUSEUM DEN HAAG   RIZZOLI ELECTA NEW YORK

IEN WHO
TIONIZED
FASHION

DIRECTOR'S FOREWORD

The Peabody Essex Museum is proud to partner with the Kunstmuseum Den Haag, which presented the first iteration of this exhibition, *Femmes Fatales: Strong Women in Fashion,* in the Netherlands in 2018. We are grateful to Benno Tempel, director of the Kunstmuseum, and his talented team for their shared enthusiasm and support—especially curator Madelief Hohé, whose insight and collaborative spirit have been invaluable to the success of the project. Our innovative colleague Petra Slinkard, The Nancy B. Putnam Curator of Fashion and Textiles at PEM, brought us the idea for this exhibition and worked with an outstanding team of staff members to extend the narrative with examples from our collection as well as loans from a number of gracious private collectors and fashion houses, thus enriching PEM's presentation with new perspectives.

Of all the arts, of all the manifestations of culture, none touches us quite the way fashion does. It envelops us intimately, providing practical protection from the elements and ensuring our comfort. Garments are also psychological armor and a social pronouncement, clothing us in the courage to launch ourselves into the day and broadcasting to the world how we would like to be seen. Before they know who we are, people around us take in what we wear: uniform or sackcloth, plumage or rags. Fashion also, of course, represents a major segment of the world economy, satisfying a seemingly inexhaustible thirst for novelty and necessity in shops and on the pages of magazines and websites.

The sheer ubiquity of the clothing around us can obscure the labor and creativity that brings it into being. Some 40 million people are employed as garment workers today—a work-force that includes some of the lowest paid laborers in the world, roughly 85 percent of whom are women. Whether in the 2017 feature film *The Phantom Thread* or the 2018 documentary *Yellow Is Forbidden*, recent examinations of haute couture make it clear that, when it comes to design and production, the business of fashion is pushed forward by the hands of countless underrecognized people, most of whom have been and continue to be women.

Made It: The Women Who Revolutionized Fashion takes a small step toward addressing the need for greater recognition of women as makers of fashion. As originated by our colleagues at the Kunstmuseum, then shown at the Modemuseum in Hasselt, Belgium, the exhibition was inspired by and celebrated the elevation of an unprecedented number of women to positions of creative control in storied European fashion houses. It also acknowledged the rising chorus of female voices declaring "Enough!" in the wake of the Me Too movement, the US Women's March of 2017, and affiliated actions. PEM's presentation augments this compelling core with distinctly American stories and perspectives.

It is entirely appropriate, then, that our presentation of this exhibition occurs in a year when we mark the centenary of the ratification of the 19th Amendment to the US Constitution, granting women the right to vote. Contemplating that hard-won landmark today, are we not pressed to ask, What took so long? The same question applies to *Made It: The Women Who Revolutionized Fashion*. This exhibition is not only about fashion design but also about acceptance—about women pushing to be seen as equals and treated fairly for their ideas, spirit, and creativity. The comprehensive history of fashion remains untold without an accounting of the contributions of women in all areas and eras: the production of textiles, notions, and findings; the design, cut, and construction of garments; the promotion, sale, and finally wear of the garments they themselves inspired. Over the last century, the design industry—especially that of the United States as it emerged from the shadow of Paris—has been dominated by women. Yet until very recently, female designers as a whole were not as readily credited or frequently recognized as their male counterparts.

One thread that runs through this book is how often the combination of women and fashion provided a spark that powered social and economic advancement—however incremental, incomplete, and belated it may have been (and continues to be). From the seventeenth-century Provençal seamstresses in Madelief Hohé's essay, who made inroads into all-male tailors' guilds to the striking New England textile workers described by Petra Slinkard, women working in the garment industry have been at the front lines in the fight for equity in labor. And as Eunice Johnson's Ebony Fashion Fairs and Maria Grazia Chiuri's redefinition of what is feminine at Dior demonstrate, women have used their influence to expand opportunity and inclusiveness in fashion.

Simply put, the designers featured here changed the way women dressed, which changed how women moved, which in turn—in time—changed *where* women moved. Consider the freedom gained as women designers shed whalebone corsets, shunned male-designed confections like the all-too-accurately named hobble skirt, and met the needs of women who were entering the workforce in ever increasing numbers and ever more diverse roles. As Rachel Syme points out in her essay, a woman designing clothing for a woman produces distinctly different results from a man doing the same. As they changed the silhouette of women's styles, these designers also changed the profile of women in business. The acumen and ambition of formidable figures such as Gabrielle Chanel, Donna Karan, and Vivienne Westwood enabled them to build empires that dominate the pages of *Vogue* to this day. Recognizing the need for change—on the runway *and* in the boardroom—they demanded it, pushed for it, and won it.

Along with the Kunstmuseum Den Haag, we are particularly indebted to lenders Jimmy Raye; Adnan Ege Kutay; Mrs. William McCormick Blair Jr.; the Chicago History Museum; the Museum of Fine Arts, Boston; Alabama Chanin; Iris van Herpen; Christian Dior; Vivienne Westwood; Katharine Hamnett; Stella McCartney; and Givenchy for their support of this exhibition. Very few exhibitions get off the ground without the kindness and generosity of individuals and companies, and *Made It: The Women Who Revolutionized Fashion* is no exception. Leslie and Angus Littlejohn, Carolyn and Peter S. Lynch and The Lynch Foundation, James B. and Mary Lou Hawkes, Henry and Callie Brauer, Jennifer and Andrew Borggaard, Kate and Ford O'Neil, and Chip and Susan Robie provided generous support. We also recognize the generosity of the East India Marine Associates of the Peabody Essex Museum and the additional support provided by MR. SID, Inc.

The women we celebrate here changed the world in ways both grand and discreet. Some of them are household names; some remain anonymous. In honoring the few, we also hope to bring attention to the hundreds of thousands of women around the globe who contribute to the industry, most of whom are and will continue to be underrepresented, underappreciated, and in many cases unseen. As we look to the future, we hope that exhibitions like *Made It: The Women Who Revolutionized Fashion* will encourage others to seek out the stories yet to be told and share them as widely as possible.

Brian P. Kennedy
The Rose-Marie and Eijk van Otterloo Director and CEO, Peabody Essex Museum

ACKNOWLEDGMENTS

No exhibition comes together in isolation, and *Made It: The Women Who Revolutionized Fashion* is no exception. The opportunity to stage this exhibition and share even a few of the stories representing some of the women who influenced the fashion industry is an honor and a privilege. I am enormously appreciative of the teams at the Peabody Essex Museum (PEM) and the Kunstmuseum Den Haag for lending their time, talent, and enduring enthusiasm to this project. We could not have done it without you.

I am especially grateful to my colleague Madelief Hohé, curator at the Kunstmuseum Den Haag, whose vision for this exhibition inspired us to share the story of strong women in fashion in the United States, as well as Benno Tempel, director of the Kunstmuseum, and Brian P. Kennedy, The Rose-Marie and Eijk van Otterloo Director and CEO, and Lynda Roscoe Hartigan, The James B. and Mary Lou Hawkes Deputy Director and Chief Curator, at PEM, for their leadership and critical guidance.

The dedicated team of people that made this publication possible includes Madelief Hohé and Rachel Syme, whose expertise and scholarship greatly expanded our narrative. I also salute my brilliant collaborators at PEM: Paula Richter, whose profound insights and deep knowledge of fashion and women's history were critical in shaping the book and exhibition, and Lan Morgan, for her keen research, organization, and embrace of the subject. I extend special thanks to our outstanding editor, Tom Fredrickson, whose patience, vision, and skill helped to shape the content of this publication, and to the book's designer, Jena Sher, for infusing the layouts with creative flair. Thank you to Kathy Fredrickson, chief of curatorial affairs, for her unwavering support and overall direction on the publication; Claire Blechman, digital asset manager, for her herculean efforts in obtaining rights and reproductions; and to Rebecca Bednarz, editor for exhibition research and publishing, for her continuous positivity, support, and guidance.

A remarkable team contributed to the presentation of the exhibition at PEM. This includes designers Dave Seibert, Lito Karatsoli-Chanikian, and Jackie Traynor, whose creative insights, resourcefulness, and imagination made the exhibition a success. Sincere thanks also go to associate director of integrated media Ed Rodley and interpretive planners Frank Redner and Liz Gardner, who lent their skill and passion for storytelling to create an enriching experience for people of all ages. Priscilla Danforth, director of exhibition planning, and Sarah Otto, exhibition planner, along with Francesca Williams,

registrar, and Amy Damon, assistant registrar, deftly and good-naturedly choreographed each stage of this project, including its movement from the Netherlands to Salem. We thank our counterparts at the Kunstmuseum, Daniel Koep, Esther van der Minne, Ap Gewald, Hanneke Modderkolk, Alice de Groot, Cesar Rodriguez Salinas, Bina Sheombar, Marije Blaasse, and Kathleen Mahieu, who were equally instrumental in facilitating both this publication and the exhibition's run at PEM. Deidre Windsor, Johanna Tower, Diane Boltz, Camille Myers Breeze, and Morgan Carbone all provided detailed assistance in conserving the garments.

Many other colleagues at PEM contributed to the success of the project, including Mic Billingsley, Caryn Boehm, Elisabeth Buell, John Childs, Jennifer Close, Kathleen Corcoran, Mollie Denhard, Rebecca Ehrhardt, Lauren Fairweather, Susan Flynn, Jen Hache, Caroline Herr, Scott Hultman, Dan Lipcan, Amanda Clark MacMullan, Megan MacNeil, Tim Merry, Brittany Minton, Karen Moreau Ceballos, Derek O'Brien, Victor Oliveira, Kristen O'Neil, Dave O'Ryan, Bob Packert, Sean Pyburn, Henry Rutkowski, Ken Sawyer, Ellen Soares, Mel Taing, Chip Van Dyke, Whitney Van Dyke, Eric Wolin, and Melissa Woods. Our many capable interns made significant contributions to help move the project forward: Sarah Goodrow, Kelsey Roebelen, Bethany McKie, Cassandra Milani, Annika Morrill, Allison Taylor, and Jillian Willis.

Many institutions, designers, and individuals graciously expanded the scope and richness of the project by lending works to the exhibition. Our special thanks go to Jimmy Raye; Adnan Ege Kutay; Mrs. William McCormick Blair Jr.; the Museum of Fine Arts, Boston; the Chicago History Museum; Alabama Chanin; Stella McCartney; Vivienne Westwood; Katharine Hamnett; Iris van Herpen; Givenchy; and Christian Dior. We are indebted to you for your generosity and enthusiastic support of this exhibition.

Petra Slinkard
The Nancy B. Putnam Curator of Fashion and Textiles
Peabody Essex Museum

WOMEN WEARING WOMEN
RACHEL SYME

Katharine Hepburn was not a sentimental person when it came to clothing. In her youth, she rarely wore the same trousers twice. In her older years, she gravitated toward a simple, workmanlike uniform, which today we might call a "capsule collection": black turtleneck, woolly slacks, a starched white oxford shirt open at the neck. In the movies, she wore beautiful gowns—slinky satin numbers cut on the bias, ornate tuffets of tulle, girlish gingham pinafores—but her body seemed to reject them offscreen. She liked to twist herself into complicated pretzels when she sat in chairs, her legs dangling off the side at odd angles. Pants were better for expanding in, for taking up space.

It is notable, then, that Hepburn allowed one hyperfeminine dress to take up space in her closet for three decades, and that she treasured it so much that she wore it in a film after all those years. The garment she kept was a voluminous pink dress made of silk organza and crepe de chine that she wore for the first time while playing the plucky socialite Tracy Lord in the 1939 Broadway production of The Philadelphia Story.

The gown, which was the color of new ballet slippers and featured a lace-up corset waist, was made for Hepburn by an eccentric Ukrainian couturiere living in New York City named Valentina (née Valentina Nikolaevna Sanina Schlee of Kiev), who created all of the costumes for the stage production. Valentina, who often modeled her own clothes and smoked cigarettes out of a dramatically long holder, never became a famous designer, though she regularly made trunks' worth of clothing for the wealthiest women in Manhattan, including the Vanderbilts and Whitneys. Her client list was small but devoted, convinced that she knew the secret to showcasing the female form. As the fashion critic Kennedy Fraser, who interviewed Valentina for the New Yorker when the designer was in her nineties, wrote: "In the way she used fabric she was often compared to a sculptor. Some of her gowns drew inspiration from the Renaissance or classical Greece. They were very simple, or looked that way. She preferred loops of self-fabric to buttons, and avoided extraneous trim."[1] In other words, like so many other women designing for women, she was a formalist. She understood women's bodies because she understood her own, and she draped fabric in flattering waves with a deliberate and knowing hand.

According to Fraser, Valentina and Hepburn grew close during the stage production of The Philadelphia Story, and even though the Hollywood costume designer Adrian swooped in to make the clothes for the film adaptation, Hepburn held a sentimental attachment to Valentina's work. In 1973 she finally found a way to wear the pink gown on screen, in the film adaptation of The Glass Menagerie. "At last," Valentina is said to have boasted about her creation, "I have made her look like a woman."[2]

What does it mean to make a woman look like a woman in clothes? This question certainly does not have one easy answer. Women are not a monolith, nor are our bodies. Still, there is an argument to be made that we, as women, intimately understand our own proportions and may have some inherent, intuitive knowledge when it comes to swaddling ourselves in fabric. It is such a basic argument—that women, knowing themselves, may in turn know best how to design clothes for other women—it seems almost ludicrous to state it. But here we are, in 2020, reckoning with the fact that over the last century so many of the designers famous for innovating women's fashion were men: Dior, Balenciaga, Saint Laurent, Lagerfeld, Givenchy, de la Renta, McQueen. Of course, there were women who broke through as a result of sheer will (Chanel, Schiaparelli, Karan, Prada) or by tragic circumstance (Donatella Versace). But for every Chanel who became a galactic brand, there is a Valentina, forgotten and overlooked, their crinolines crumbling in an attic somewhere.

In an ideal world an exhibition like Made It: The Women Who Revolutionized Fashion would not be radical. The many groundbreaking contributions women have made to how we dress and how we experience our clothing would be less a shadow history and more a lingua franca. Elsa Schiaparelli's hot pink once shocked consumers, but her contributions to consumer culture should no longer feel shocking. And yet we are still engaged in an ongoing process of recovering the work of the women who dressed women, who forged new ground in fashion because they desired their own bodies to take new shapes and then made those shapes possible.

·

In French, the word soeurs means sisters, and it was important to the sisters Callot that the word—so familial, so feminine—be sewn into every dress they made. The house of Callot Soeurs was opened in 1895 in Paris by four daughters—Marie, Marthe, Régine, Joséphine—of a lacemaker and an engraver, although they became most famous for dressing high-society doyennes as a trio (Joséphine killed herself two years into the business, a traumatic event we still know little about). The sisters' shop, which began as a place to buy notions (high-end ribbons, feathers, delicate broderie anglaise lace) grew into one of the most powerful outfitters of wealthy women in France, swelling to several hundred employees. The Callot sisters mentored and promoted several women who went on to have an impact on the way other women dressed, including the seamstress Madeleine Vionnet, who would establish her own house in Paris in 1912 and became famous for her structured gowns that fell across the hips on the bias, and Georgette Renal, who would go on to win the competition to make the first in-flight hostess outfits for Air France in 1942, a navy wool suit nipped at the waist and paired with a crisp white poplin shirt.

The Callot Soeurs dresses in this exhibition (pp. 42–43) are from the mid-1920s, and they are typical of the silhouettes favored at that time by flappers and flapper hangers-on: dropped waist, loose around the hips, practically melting off the shoulders. But there is something about each piece that is rare, and idiosyncratic. The beaded open-back gown, from 1920–24, falls down the body like a weighted lure, the heft of its intricate embellishments automatically preventing any cling or awkward angles. Along with the thin matching scarf that runs down the back like an untied bow tie resting around the neck of a tuxedo shirt at the end of the night, the dress is exceptionally flattering and feminine while still retaining a hint of androgyny. The other Callot Soeurs evening gown here—a cream-and-poppy-colored floral silk creation from around 1925—features a geometric, asymmetrical handkerchief hemline that feels less jazz club than it does Studio 54. Both pieces were of their time—Callot Soeurs, like so many fashion houses of the early twentieth century, made most of their profits catering to debutantes and heiresses, a client base that not only craved what was in vogue but whose pampered lives revolved around chasing aesthetic novelty—but also strangely ahead of it. It is as if the woman, or women, who designed these dresses were performing a subtle trick to fling the garments past the current moment; the work conforms to trends but also elides them, puts the body before the fad. The beaded dress, because of its weight, scoops down in the back in an alluring, crisp triangle, just barely exposing the scapulae. This contour is so legibly seductive that it tantalizes even the contemporary eye.

It is possible, viewing these garments, to see why Callot Soeurs' customers were so loyal to the house. In the 1990s

art historian cataloguing a large cache of classical paintings at the ornate Italian mansion Villa La Pietra—which once belonged to an American antiques dealer named Arthur Acton and his much-wealthier wife, Hortense Lenore Mitchell Acton, whose father was president of the Illinois Trust and Savings Bank during the Gilded Age—came across a strange discovery. She found several Louis Vuitton steamer trunks filled with lavish evening gowns, all by the same designer. According to the journalist Jessamyn Hatcher, who is currently writing a biography of the Callot sisters and wrote about the discovery of the trunks in the New Yorker, the historian at the villa stumbled upon "a collection of exquisite dresses, the kind usually seen only in movies, or inside protective vitrines in museums. Closer inspection revealed silk labels, hand-woven with the name 'Callot Soeurs.'" As it turns out, Hortense Acton was intensely devoted to the house of Callot, to the point where she owned over twenty custom pieces—many of which are now housed in institutions like the Kunstmuseum Den Haag and the Peabody Essex Museum. She found that the seamstresses in their Parisian atelier most understood how to make her feel like a sumptuous woman; how, in dropping the strictures of the corset and experimenting with looser waists and unusual hemlines, they allowed women to begin defining for themselves what constituted luxury and personal style. Vionnet always credited the house with teaching her how to look beyond fashion as chassis construction and to see how it could ascend into the realm of art: "Without the example of the Callot Soeurs, I would have continued to make Fords. It is because of them that I have been able to make Rolls-Royces."[3]

•

What do women see when they look at other women's bodies? One may think that the eye may tilt immediately toward envy, toward comparison. But perhaps a better word for the transference that can sometimes take place is desire; there is an erotic kind of looking that can happen between women, and it is even more charged when it comes to clothes. We see another's plumage and imagine how it would feel against our own skin, what kind of person we might be if we walked a mile in another's sequins. What women designers of all eras have learned to do is to turn that desire into craftsmanship. They've made their innate longing productive.

This does not mean that all women desire the same way or yearn for the same things. It is just that women fashion designers seem to know how to give a woman what she wants before she knows it, in a way that feels almost symbiotic and sui generis, versus so many of the harsh and willfully provocative silhouettes invented by male designers who see the female body as a moving dress form for experimentation. That kind of design is external, imposed upon. The design innovations that have come from women—be it Donna Karan's creation of the capsule collection, Hanae Mori's playful use of textiles, Vivienne Westwood's punkish bat-wing blazers, Ann Demeulemeester's gothic black woolens, Miuccia Prada's reclamation of classical Italian suiting, Phoebe Philo's minimalist neutral cottons, or Rei Kawakubo's grandiose forays into fantastical, and sometimes even ugly, deconstructivism— feel almost as if they begin from the inside out. The clothes don't exist to shape the woman; the woman exists to shape the clothes.

What does it feel like to move through the world in clothes designed by a woman's hand? There is no simple answer to this question, but there is some deeper form of communion to be had. When Valentina made Hepburn "look like a woman," what she may have been saying is that she created a dress that the movie star would want to keep and return to again and again, not out of some maudlin attachment, but because it was a garment that made her feel like *herself*. She highlighted some core aspect of Hepburn's sense of glamour—that pink dress, at that exact moment—that stayed fused to the actress, such that she was compelled to trot it out again in her final years as a kind of sartorial closure.

The garments in this exhibition are as different from one another as women are. You can use them to chart the history of fashion, from boned corsets to bouclé suits to Chromat's fetishistic harnesses, but they don't tell just one, linear story. Moving through the show, you'll find that what the pieces have most in common is that they show women in every era grappling with their *own* bodies, pushing against their own limitations. It's a time capsule of every time a woman has looked into a mirror and, in an effort to connect more deeply with the reflection she sees, got to work.

1 Kennedy Fraser, *Ornament and Silence: Essays on Women's Lives* (New York: Vintage, 1996), 171.
2 Fraser, *Ornament and Silence*, 179.
3 Jessamyn Hatcher, "Portfolio: Twenty-One Dresses," *New Yorker*, March 23, 2015, https://www.newyorker.com/magazine/2015/03/23/twenty-one-dresses.

ALTERING THE PATTERN
CHANGING TIMES
AND NEW ROLES IN FASHION
MADELIEF HOHÉ

Mantua, about 1760–65, Kunstmuseum Den Haag, 0555918

revolution started in 1652 when male tailors in Aix-en-Provence admitted female seamstresses to their guild. Tailoring had been a male occupation from time immemorial, and guilds—which supported and regulated their profession and standards of craftsmanship—had been dominated by men since the Middle Ages. Regulations varied by town, country, and period, but in general male townsmen ran the guilds. Membership was determined by such factors as education, skill, and religion (Jews were excluded in the Netherlands, as were Catholics after the Reformation), as well as gender.

The tailor—*tailleur* in French, from *tailler*, meaning "to cut"— was held in high esteem because the cutting of fabric was considered a skill requiring special expertise and knowledge. This had to do with the fact that textiles were extremely expensive. A customer would purchase material from a fabric merchant and bring it to a tailor to have clothing made. If it was not cut correctly, the mistake could cost the tailor a lot of money. The work of the seamstress—*couturière*, from *coudre*, "to sew"—involved draping, folding, and sewing the cut fabric to achieve the desired shape. This role was considered subservient to that of the tailor, with seamstresses earning less than and working "in the service of" tailors or independently (sometimes illegally) and without the support of a professional guild.

That changed in 1675 when seamstresses in Paris and Rouen organized their own professional guilds.[1] Membership in the Paris guild grew quickly: eighty-two head seamstresses were admitted in the first year, and by 1691 the organization boasted a thousand members. The Paris and Rouen guilds were unique in Europe; in other cities the situation remained as it had for centuries. While some towns in the Netherlands had previously permitted mixed membership, during the course of the seventeenth century the guilds became an exclusively male bailiwick.[2]

In France and the Netherlands seamstresses specialized as either wool seamstresses, who created outer clothing for women and children, or linen seamstresses, who dealt with undergarments and trousseaus. Of the two groups, the linen seamstresses had the lower status; if they lacked work, they often had to resort to prostitution—a widely known circumstance that resulted in ambiguous depictions in literature.[3] When the wool seamstresses formed a guild, they were barred from making men's clothes and clothing for boys older than eight years (the age they started to wear breeches) and were permitted to make only certain types of women's and children's garments.[4] For example, court dress for women, consisting of a boned bodice (*corps de robe* with whalebone), skirt, and train—the most luxurious and prestigious form of female fashion—was the preserve of tailors.[5] They were thus often described as *tailleurs d'habits d'hommes et de corps de femmes et enfants*

(tailors for male costumes and boned bodices for women and children). For centuries it was evidently inconceivable that women might make men's clothes professionally. The types of garments that female seamstresses were permitted to make— the manteau, for example, a robe worn with a petticoat and an unboned bodice with an overskirt trained at the back— involved simpler techniques and relied more on folding and draping than court dress with stays.

But nothing is so fickle as fashion. Whenever a new form or item of clothing became popular, the question of who was permitted to make it, the tailor or the seamstress, arose anew. This was the case with a new type of women's gown that emerged at the end of the seventeenth century, the mantua (from *manteau*). This dress, which featured a draped overgarment, developed into a loosely hanging gown with a belt. Seamstresses in England were so linked with this style that they were known as "mantua makers." As production of this item was not restricted to tailors, seamstresses appropriated it for themselves, just as they did with the so-called whalebone skirt, a type of hoop skirt that came into fashion around

Madame La Duchesse de Vantadour dressed in a mantua, around 1690, Kunstmuseum Den Haag

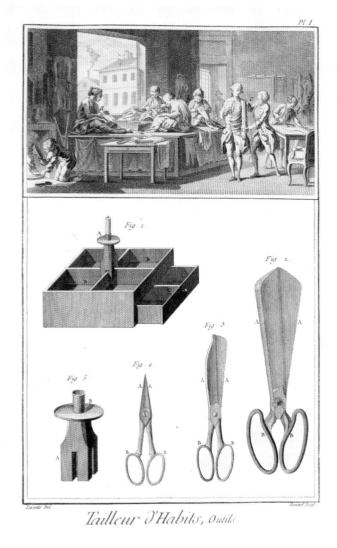

"Tailleur d'habits," from *Encyclopédie, ou dictionnaire raisonné des sciences, des arts et des métiers*, ed. Denis Diderot and Jean le Rond d'Alembert (Paris, 1751–72)

the production of women's and children's clothing and would even be permitted to make several types of men's garments.[8] The dam had burst. In just one hundred years, these female professionals had largely dethroned male tailors in the design and production of clothing for women and children.

This victory was short-lived, however, as guilds were abolished in France in 1791, during the Revolution, and in the Netherlands in 1818.[9] After this, anyone—male or female—could make and sell anything they wanted with impunity. Naturally, this boosted competition in a fashion industry that had grown significantly over the course of the eighteenth century. Various new professions in which women were to play a prominent role had emerged during this time. Evolving from the guild of *merchants mercers*—dealers in luxury goods they themselves did not produce—were the female *marchandes de modes*. These fashion merchants sold decorations for gowns that were not made from the fabric of gowns, which was, of course, the domain of the seamstress.[10] In 1776 the *marchandes de modes* joined forces to found their own guild and made a name for themselves through their charmingly furnished shops full of attractive adornments—ribbons, bows, and other decorative items—for women's and children's clothes.[11] One such merchant was Rose Bertin, who would become known as the *ministre de la mode* (fashion minister) of Marie Antoinette. Possessing a bold personality and a gift for self-promotion that anticipated that of Gabrielle Chanel by a century, Bertin was far from the only famous *marchande de modes*. (A Madame Alexandre enjoyed a similar level of fame at the time but has since been largely forgotten.) These fashion merchants were considered "creative and unique," and they portrayed themselves as blessed with "talent" rather than occupying a profession.[12] In other words, their status as creative designers was noted and appreciated, in contrast to seamstresses or tailors, who were admired for their craftsmanship.

This recognition of creativity would transform the field of fashion in the nineteenth century. As the guilds disappeared, more and more women worked as *couturières*. Yet it took the Englishman Charles Frederick Worth to "upgrade" this profession. Worth had worked for many years in the textile trade in Paris before establishing a fashion house in 1858.[13] He understood his role as a creative one and prided himself on his artistic skills. Worth called himself a *couturier*, a word derived from the feminine *couturière*. Why this term instead of tailor? It is quite possible it had to do with the fact that the role of the tailor had lost its masculine value over the course of the eighteenth century. For example, in *Émile* (1762), French philosopher Jacques Rousseau agitated against men performing "women's work" (*métiers de femmes*) like sewing and embroidery: "The needle and the sword cannot be manipulated by the

1717 along with another wide dress, the *robe volante*, likewise quite loose in its cut. Tailors had the right to make the stays and *corps*, or bodice with boning, so they believed that they—and not seamstresses—had the right to create this new type of clothing.

Emotions about this matter ran so high in Paris that in 1725, when it became known that the seamstress Marie Thérèse Sermoise was working improperly with bone, a group of tailors assaulted her in her house, causing her to miscarry.[6] Soon thereafter it was decided that seamstresses would be permitted to work with whalebone stays but not to make farthingales or panniers (variations on the hoop skirt) or *emboutissures* (which involved inserting stays into a bodice).[7] In 1727, however, seamstresses were granted the right to make skirts, panniers, and hoop skirts with whalebone stays. As the years passed, further rights were awarded to the seamstresses. They achieved a great triumph in 1781 when it was declared that seamstresses would henceforth have a monopoly on

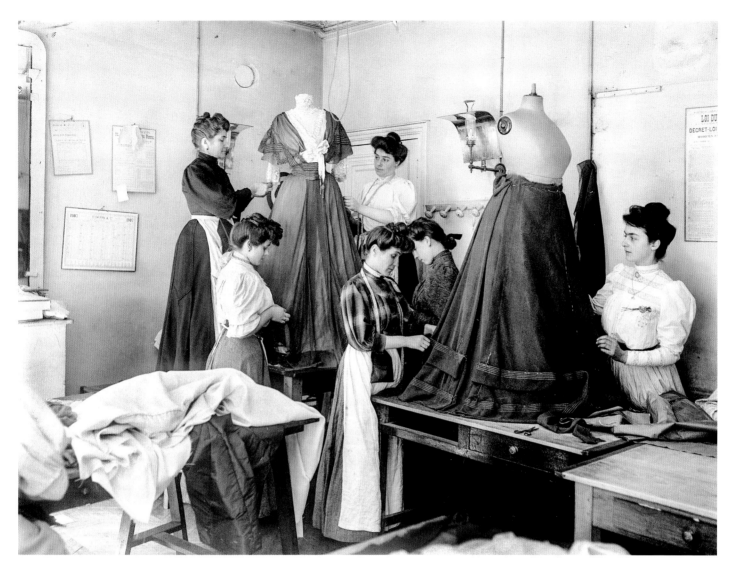

Seamstresses at work in the atelier of Charles Frederick Worth, 1907

same hands."[14] Furthermore, the profession of tailor was associated mainly with craftsmanship and not with creativity—the very quality that Worth felt distinguished him. One way Worth expressed his status was to sign his creations like a true artist, sewing his name into the waistband of his gowns, the first designer to do so.

The nineteenth-century couturier shed the traditional modesty of the tailor and emerged as a self-proclaimed creative genius. Within the ever-growing luxury industry, the couturier supplied custom-made clothing for women in which vision was prized above all other traits.[15] This made the position of women working as *couturières* still more difficult: they continued to be regarded as "simple seamstresses," while their male colleagues were deemed "world-famous artists and businessmen."[16] Unlike the tailor or seamstress, who merely made clothing, the couturier dictated what his clients wore. As Worth's example was imitated by flamboyant characters such as Jacques Doucet and Paul Poiret, the status of couturiers grew. By the early twentieth century, the craft of the tailor

had become completely overshadowed by the imagination of the couturier.

It is remarkable, then, that women were involved in starting their own fashion houses right from the start, at a time when members of their sex were officially "legally incompetent" under the Napoleonic Code. One of these women was Jeanne Paquin, who opened her atelier in 1891. Madeleine Vionnet followed suit in 1912, around the time that Jeanne Lanvin and Chanel turned their attention from millinery to clothes. But men so dominated the fashion world that creative female designers like Vionnet and Chanel were often dismissed; it is no coincidence that Poiret referred to Chanel as "that seamstress" when he wanted to offend her, marking a sharp contrast to his own persona as a great couturier. Despite such slights, the 1920s and 1930s proved to be a golden age for female designers. The name best remembered now is Chanel, as famous for her innovative designs as for her striking personality, but at the time she was just one of many female designers. Her contemporary Jeanne Adèle Bernard Sacerdote,

Chiara Ferragni in Dior, Paris Fashion Week, 2017

founder of the house of Jenny, is now largely forgotten, yet she—along with Paquin, Lanvin, and Vionnet—enjoyed just as much prestige as Chanel at the time. Various sets of sisters also joined forces and set up successful houses, such as the Callot Soeurs and Boué Soeurs.

·

Another sort of revolution was launched in fall 2016 when Maria Grazia Chiuri presented her first ready-to-wear collection for Dior. The Spring 2017 collection marked the seventieth anniversary of Christian Dior's landmark inaugural collection, now universally known as the "New Look." After Dior's death in 1957, the house continued under the leadership of a series of designers, all of them men.[17] Chiuri was the first female designer to take the helm—as her first collection made clear. Taking the classic Dior "New Look" as a starting point, Chiuri modernized it by making skirts transparent and putting them over Dior-logo panties and by combining the classic Dior Bar Jacket with simple T-shirts bearing slogans such as "(Dio)Revolution" and "We Should All Be Feminists." The latter phrase comes from a TEDx talk and essay by the Nigerian writer and activist Chimamanda Ngozi Adichie, who called for "a world of happier men and happier women who are truer to themselves. And this is how to start: we must raise our daughters differently. We must also raise our sons differently."[18]

Chiuri said she felt the need to speak out about the US presidential campaign that resulted in the election of Donald Trump in 2016. "The more I read and learn about the world, the more there is to say," said Chiuri. "I've realized that fashion is a very powerful medium."[19] And this realization shaped her approach to Dior's designs:

Dior is feminine. That's what I kept hearing when I told people I was coming here. But as a woman, "feminine" means something different to me than it means to a man, perhaps. Feminine is about being a woman, no? I thought to myself: If Dior is about femininity, then it is about women. And not about what it was to be a woman fifty years ago, but to be a woman today . . . When you are a woman making clothes for women, then fashion is not just about how you look. It is about how you feel and how you think.[20]

A variety of social actions materialized following the 2016 election: the women's marches in January 2017, for example, and the debut of the pink "pussy" hat as a symbol of female solidarity (and which Angela Missoni immediately included in her Autumn 2017 runway collection for Missoni) and the increasing momentum of the #MeToo and #TimesUp movements protesting sexual abuse and harassment.[21] In Dior's Spring 2018 collection, Chiuri posed another provocative question with a T-shirt reading "Why Are There No Great Women Artists?" Here the reference was to Linda Nochlin's landmark 1971 essay of that title. At the 2018 Golden Globe Awards most female attendees wore black as a nonverbal expression of unity. Oprah Winfrey, dressed in a black evening gown by Donatella Versace, gave a striking speech: "I want all the girls watching here and now to know that a new day is on the horizon! And when that new day finally dawns, it will be because of a lot of magnificent women, many of whom are right here in this room tonight, and some pretty phenomenal men, fighting hard to make sure that they become the leaders who take us to the time when nobody ever has to say 'Me Too' again."[22]

The debut of Chiuri's Dior collection and the events that inspired and surrounded it led the Kunstmuseum Den Haag to consider an exhibition focusing exclusively on female fashion designers—its first ever. Never before had so many female designers been in command of fashion houses. Consider Phoebe Philo, who was at Céline; Miuccia Prada; Sarah Burton at Alexander McQueen; Iris van Herpen; and, of course, Rei Kawakubo at Comme des Garçons and Vivienne Westwood—women who are regarded as some of the most important fashion designers of the twentieth century. These designers are powerful women, and some of them are very vocal on political or feminist issues. Female designers are also stimulating innovation in the industry—like van Herpen, who experiments with 3-D printing and other new technologies, and Rei Kawakubo, who swathes the female body in extreme shapes according to her own unique aesthetic. Not long after the concept of the exhibition was born, Givenchy appointed its first female leader, Clare Waight Keller.

We wanted to address three key questions in the exhibition: Do female designers design differently for women than their male colleagues? How does being a woman affect their creations? What is their vision of fashion? There are, of course, no simple answers, and it is dangerous to generalize. But it is certainly striking that many female designers work on the "hand, heart, and head" principle. Hands, because many of them care deeply about the technical design process and shape their material by hand around the female body. Heart, because they work from feelings and attach great importance to mobility, physicality, and comfortable fit. And head, because many female designers use clothes as a medium to express their (social) opinions; in addition, some of these designers create very conceptual works that depart from conventions and shun the so-called male gaze, thus dressing women without objectifying them.

At long last, the time is ripe to celebrate *The Women Who Revolutionized Fashion*.

1 Clare Haru Crowston, *Fabricating Women: The Seamstresses of Old Regime France, 1675–1791* (Durham, NC: Duke University Press, 2001), 1.
2 An exception was Amsterdam, where in 1579 wool seamstresses united but officially remained dues-paying members of the tailors' guild. Bibi Panhuysen, *Maatwerk: kleermakers, naaisters, oudkleerkopers en de gilden (1500–1800)* [Customization: tailors, dressmakers, old-fashioned buyers, and the guilds (1500–1800)] (Amsterdam: Stichting beheer IISG, 2000), 205–06.
3 Panhuysen, *Maatwerk*, 188.
4 Crowston, *Fabricating Women*, 3. Could this explain the custom by which boys were "breeched"—dressed in trousers, like men, for the first time—when they turned seven or eight? In other words, is it possible that boys wore skirts as long as they were dressed by female seamstresses (who were not trained to cut and sew trousers) and only received their first trousers at the age of seven or eight when they went to a male tailor? This hypothesis has yet to be addressed in the literature, but investigations such as Crowston's *Fabricating Women* and Panhuysen's *Maatwerk* have only recently detailed the world of the seamstress and tailor. For more on this subject, see Saskia Kuus, "Rokkekinderen in de Nederlanden, 1560–1660: Een onderzoek naar het verschil in kleding tussen meisjes en jongens in rokken" [Childrenswear in the Netherlands, 1560–1660: an investigation into the difference in clothing between girls and boys in skirts], *Kostuum* (1994): 6–13; and Saskia Kuus, "Kinderen op hun mooist: Kinderkleding in de zestiende en zeventiende eeuw" [Children at their best: children's clothing in the sixteenth and seventeenth centuries], in *Kinderen op hun mooist: Het kinderportret in de Nederlanden, 1500–1700* [Children at their best: children's portraits in the Netherlands, 1500–1700], ed. Jean Baptist Bedaux and Rudi Ekkart (Ghent: Ludion, 2000).
5 Crowston, *Fabricating Women*, 31, 36.
6 Crowston, *Fabricating Women*, 55.
7 Crowston, *Fabricating Women*, 56, 57.
8 Crowston, *Fabricating Women*, 66.
9 Panhuysen, *Maatwerk*, 5.
10 Crowston, *Fabricating Women*, 67.
11 Crowston, *Fabricating Women*, 68.
12 Crowston, *Fabricating Women*, 68.
13 Worth initially launched a fashion house with his business partner Otto Bobergh as Worth & Bobergh; he later worked under his name only. Diana de Marly, *Worth: Father of Haute Couture* (London: Holmes & Meier, 1980), 31.
14 Crowston, *Fabricating Women*, 1.
15 Crowston, *Fabricating Women*, 2, 65.
16 Crowston, *Fabricating Women*, 2.
17 Yves Saint Laurent (1957–60), Marc Bohan (1960–89), Gianfranco Ferré (1989–97), John Galliano (1997–2011), and Raf Simons (2012–15).
18 Chimamanda Ngozi Adichie, "We Should All Be Feminists," filmed December 2012 in London, TEDxEuston video, 29:21, https://www.ted.com/talks/chimamanda_ngozi_adichie_we_should_all_be_feminists?language=en. Chimamanda Ngozi Adichie, *We Should All Be Feminists* (London: Fourth Estate, 2014).
19 Lisa Armstrong, "'I didn't really discover feminism until I was 48': Dior's Maria Grazia Chiuri on Using Fashion for Political Ends," *Daily Telegraph*, November 29, 2017, https://www.telegraph.co.uk/fashion/people/didnt-really-discover-feminism-48-diors-maria-grazia-chiuri/.
20 Jess Cartner-Morley, "Maria Chiuri on Fashion, Feminism, and Dior: 'You Must Fight for Your Ideas,'" *The Fashion, The Guardian* and *The Observer's* biannual fashion supplement, March 18, 2017, https://www.theguardian.com/fashion/2017/mar/18/maria-grazia-chiuri-fashionfeminism-fight-for-ideas.
21 While "Me Too" and #MeToo gained broader notoriety in 2017, the movement was begun in 2006 by Bronx-based civil rights activist Tarana Burke. https://en.wikipedia.org/wiki/Tarana_Burke.
22 Giovanni Russonello, "Read Oprah Winfrey's Golden Globes Speech," *New York Times*, January 7, 2018, https://www.nytimes.com/2018/01/07/movies/oprah-winfrey-golden-globesspeech-transcript.html.

AT THE CUTTING EDGE
AMERICAN FASHION
AS CATALYST FOR CHANGE

PETRA SLINKARD

n May 1824, 102 women between the ages of fifteen and thirty employed as textile weavers in Pawtucket, Rhode Island, launched the first major factory strike in American history—and the first anywhere led by women. The strike was called in reaction to the decision by mill owners to increase the length of the workday for all employees in Pawtucket's textile factories while decreasing the pay for power-loom weavers, all of whom were women. In factories where jobs were organized by gender, women weavers must have seemed like easy targets. The owners justified their stance by arguing that female mill workers were already making "extravagant wages for young women" and assumed that the women would passively accept the terms. They did not. The strike went on through June and ultimately drove mill owners to make concessions. Nothing like this had occurred in America's young textile industry, and it was just the beginning.[1]

The Pawtucket strike is an early instance of how closely interwoven the textile and clothing industries were with women's efforts to secure opportunity, fairness, and something approaching equality in the United States. Time and again, the creative and industrial evolution of fashion ran on a parallel track with the broadening of rights for women. Take, for example, the first wave of feminist activism in the nineteenth century: The 1848 Seneca Falls Convention in upstate New York, the first publicly recognized women's rights gathering in the United States, called for equality between the sexes and passed a resolution urging women to secure the vote. In a related effort, the international rational dress movement rejected tight, corseted fashions and championed the wearing of full trousers, gathered and secured at the ankle—now best known as bloomers—under shorter dresses.[2] Though not the first time that dress had served as a symbol and catalyst for change, it was certainly one of the most memorable—and, it turns out, representative of a dynamic at play throughout American history.

The textile industry was one of the first to employ women and girls, being a short leap and a logical progression from the traditional domestic tasks of weaving and sewing. By 1830, 60 percent of the textile workers in the United States were women, and by 1837 roughly 18,000 women were employed in New England's shoe- and boot-manufacturing industry. These women embraced the opportunity for independence—sometimes necessarily, as they were increasingly depended upon to support extended families or lead single-parent households.[3] But with the good also came the bad: the hours were long, the working conditions were unsafe and in some cases unhealthy, pay was low, and women were frequently subjected to ridicule and harassment from predominately male foremen. But as women established themselves as a reliable and instrumental force in the country's burgeoning fashion industry, they were able to leverage their position to address labor

reforms. Women were hungry for change, but it came slowly and at a cost.

Between 1880 and 1930 the number of American women joining the urban workforce nearly doubled. By 1891 the number of women working outside the home had grown to 5.3 million, and the number of shirtwaist factories in New York City alone numbered around 450. In 1908, eighty-four years after the Pawtucket strike, 15,000 female garment workers marched in New York, demanding higher pay, shorter hours, voting rights, and the abolition of child labor.

In 1911, 145 mostly non-English-speaking immigrant women and children died after a fire broke out in the Triangle Shirtwaist Factory building in Manhattan. The tragedy brought widespread attention to the dangers of sweatshops and led to the passage of a series of laws and regulations improving safety for workers. The following year, 20,000 textile workers employed at the American Woolen Company went on strike in Lawrence, Massachusetts, in what is now known as the Bread and Roses Strike. After months of violent altercations, Congress investigated the causes and details of the conflict, which finally led to a settlement that granted many of the strikers' demands. Through these dangerous times, women helped to revolutionize an industry and set standards for production that have carried through to the present day.

Gains on the design side of the industry came less through collective action than through individual women seizing the chance when it arrived. In the mid-1800s, Englishman Charles Frederick Worth rose to fame in Paris as the dressmaker of choice for the French court, opening his house in 1858 and establishing a new foundation for the French fashion industry. In 1860, an ocean away, a recently self-liberated enslaved black woman and single mother named Elizabeth Keckley opened a dressmaking business in Washington, DC. She quickly became the go-to designer for the American political and social elite and served as the personal dresser and couturiere to Mary Todd Lincoln. While the French and American capitals differed greatly, the level of skill and quality of design required to satisfy their demanding clienteles didn't. Although Worth has been lauded in fashion history as the "father of haute couture," Keckley has, until very recently, been all but absent.

Keckley wasn't the only woman making her way in the United States. In 1859 a New England dressmaker and milliner known as Madame Demorest invented mass-produced tissue-paper dressmaking patterns. Her patterns made French styles accessible to ordinary women, thus greatly influencing US fashion. *Demorest's Illustrated Monthly Magazine* and *Mme. Demorest's Mirror of Fashions* sold millions of copies and empowered home sewers all over the United States. Women were also making strides elsewhere, albeit slowly. The retail industry was one of the most "respectable" professions open to young women,

Women workers at a shoe factory in Haverhill, Massachusetts, 1920

but rarely did they advance beyond selling products on the floor. In 1866, however, a woman from Nantucket, Massachusetts, named Margaret Getchell became the first retail executive at Macy's department store in New York when she was promoted to the position of superintendent.

Fifty-five years later Getchell would be followed by another retail trailblazer. Dorothy Shaver started her career as a teacher in Arkansas but was fired in 1914 when she and three other women attended a dance unchaperoned. Through a series of circuitous events, Shaver in 1921 found herself employed at New York's Lord & Taylor, where she went on to become one of the most notable female executives in American retail history. In 1930 Shaver, along with Edna Woolman Chase (editor in chief of *Vogue*), Elizabeth Arden, Helena Rubenstein, designers Adele Simpson and Clare Potter, and eleven other women (including Eleanor Roosevelt) launched the Fashion Group (now the Fashion Group International) as a networking organization to support and guide women in the industry. Among Shaver's groundbreaking innovations were her creatively planned and

executed display windows, her treatment of employees (she was an early proponent of long maternity leaves), and her efforts to revolutionize the perception of a distinctly American style, notably through her 1932 American Look program.

Since the time of Worth, the American fashion industry had been taking its cues from Paris, with hundreds of thousands of dressmaking shops in cities across the United States employing talented designers to re-create Parisian styles. With the onset of World War II, however, Shaver astonished the fashion world when she created a campaign promoting the work of relatively unknown American designers. This bold move challenged the status quo and the industry's historical reliance on European fashion leadership. The American Look established Shaver as a department store executive with vision and foresight and exemplified not only her business acumen but also her confidence in the creativity of her peers. She put American designers on a pedestal and in the spotlight for the first time. Between 1932 and 1939 the American Look introduced more than sixty young designers, including Elizabeth Hawes, Muriel

Two women picketing at the Ladies Tailors strike, New York City, 1910

King, Edith Ruess, Nettie Rosenstein, and Lilly Dache. The clothing lines they designed for Lord & Taylor were fitted to American lifestyles: moderately priced, well constructed, and suited to casual living. As a result of her efforts, Shaver was promoted to vice president and in 1945 succeeded Walter Hoving as president of Lord & Taylor, earning the highest salary on record for any American woman at the time.[4]

Eleanor Lambert, a contemporary of Shaver's, worked as a publicist for some of fashion's greatest designers. She went on to help establish the Costume Institute at the Metropolitan Museum of Art and in 1943 laid the foundation for what is now known as New York Fashion Week.[5] Lambert wholeheartedly believed in the promise of the American garment industry and sought to establish it in a manner that would rival its international counterparts. In 1962 she founded the Council of Fashion Designers of America, with the mission "to strengthen the impact of American fashion in the global economy." In 1973 Lambert and French curator Gerald Van der Kemp envisioned an event to raise funds for the restoration of the palace at Versailles. The event, known as the Battle of Versailles, pitted American designers (Oscar de la Renta, Stephen Burrows, Halston, Bill Blass, and Anne Klein, with her assistant Donna Karan) against their French counterparts. The Parisians scoffed,

thinking the Americans would fail with their showcase of sportswear, but, in fact, the Americans stole the show.[6] They not only used eleven black models—an unprecedented number at the time—but their presentations were fun, youthful, and fresh. The show was a great triumph and solidified the importance and impact of American design in international fashion.

Another woman to use fashion shows to break new ground was Eunice Johnson. Along with her husband, John H. Johnson, she helped create the publishing empire that included *Ebony* and *Jet* magazines. In 1958 Johnson began sponsoring a charitable traveling fashion show, the Ebony Fashion Fair, that featured black designers and models to raise money for causes related to the black community. It would eventually be presented in thirty cities and become one of *the* fashion events of the year and was dubbed the "world's largest traveling fashion show." When Johnson found it difficult to borrow clothing for her shows, she bought pieces outright—and would go on to accumulate one of the best collections of haute couture in the United States as a result. She used her magazines to recruit young models and provided every attendee of her fashion shows with a free one-year subscription to *Ebony*.[7] Over the last ten years, as increasing attention has been paid to diversity on the runway—including but not limited to race, gender

Dorothy Shaver (center) reviews designs at Lord & Taylor, 1945

The Battle of Versailles, a gala and fashion show organized for the restoration of the palace at Versailles, France, 1973

identity, and ability—Johnson has been justly viewed as a pioneer, paving the way for many black models to break into the mainstream in the mid- to late twentieth century.

Wishing to promote American fashion and encourage design during World War II, the cosmetics and perfume company Coty Inc. founded the Coty American Fashion Critics' Awards in 1942. The first award was given to American designer Norman Norell, who cut his teeth under Hattie Carnegie, a savvy entrepreneur who had a knack for selecting and grooming young talent. While some of the designers who worked for Carnegie will likely never be known by name, her protégées included such powerhouses as Pauline Trigère and Claire McCardell. From 1943 to 1963 women designers received more than half of the Coty awards, including trend-setters like McCardell, Trigère, Bonnie Cashin, Tina Leser, Vera Maxwell, Anne Klein, and Adele Simpson. In a perplexing

turn, that trend waned in the 1970s and 1980s throughout the industry, with male designers reaping an increasing number of accolades. By the turn of the twenty-first century the scales seemed to be tipping back again as women designers continue to make names for themselves. More and more women are using fashion as a means to break new ground and challenge the establishment—often democratizing fashion even as they reach new peaks of creativity and innovation. Designers like Carla Fernández, Stella McCartney, Vivienne Westwood, and Natalie Chanin are calling attention to sustainability in a business that historically has been one of the most heavily polluting industries in the world.[8] In 2015 Amber Dawn-Bear Robe (Siksika Nation) established a haute couture fashion show at the annual Santa Fe Indian Market to promote and support Indigenous designers like Patricia Michaels (Taos Pueblo), Jamie Okuma (Luiseño/Shoshone-Bannock), and Sho Sho Esquiro (Kaska

Dene/Cree), while designers like Kathleen Kye and Becca McCharen-Tran are using their brands as a means to promote inclusivity and body positivity.

The road traveled by each of these women is unique. Some worked over decades, while others took the stage for just a brief moment. Some were born into privilege, using their position to make statements on the status of women and dress, while others overcame steep obstacles to achieve success. They all understood that fashion is much more than just the production of clothing. It extends beyond dresses and gowns into accessories, millinery, jewelry, and beauty products—all created to augment and modify people's appearances according to social mores, trends, or personal desires. Fashion is a powerful tool for connection and, in the hands of these women, a potent symbol of self-actualization and change.

A model at the Ebony Fashion Fair, Denver, 2004

1 Berenice Carroll, "'Shut Down the Mills!': Women, the Modern Strike, and Revolution," *The Public i* (Urbana-Champaign, IL), March 2012, http://publici.ucimc.org/2012/03/shut-down-the-mills-women-the-modern-strike-and-revolution/.
2 Sally Roesch Wagner, ed., *The Women's Suffrage Movement* (New York: Penguin Classics, 2019).
3 Joanne J. Meyerowitz, *Women Adrift: Independent Wage Earners in Chicago, 1880–1930*, Women in Culture and Society (Chicago: University of Chicago Press, 1988).
4 Sandra Lee Braun, "Forgotten First Lady: The Life, Rise, and Success of Dorothy Shaver, President of Lord & Taylor Department Store, and America's 'First Lady of Retailing,'" PhD diss., University of Alabama, 2013.
5 Jane Mulvagh, "Obituary: Eleanor Lambert," *The Independent*, October 9, 2003, https://www.independent.co.uk/news/obituaries/eleanor-lambert-37241.html.
6 Daniel James Cole and Nancy Deihl, *The History of Modern Fashion* (London: King, 2015).
7 Joy L. Bivins and Rosemary K. Adams, eds. *Inspiring Beauty: 50 Years of Ebony Fashion Fair* (Chicago: Chicago History Museum, 2013).
8 Madelief Hohé, *Femmes Fatales: Strong Women in Fashion* (The Hague: Gemeentemuseum Den Haag; Hasselt, Belgium: Modemuseum, 2018).

THE WOMEN WHO REVOLUTIONIZED FASHION

Designer profiles have been written by Petra Slinkard (PS),
Paula B. Richter (PBR), and Lan Morgan (LM).

In a project celebrating the women in fashion, we confront
the fact that many female designers have not received
adequate—or any—credit for their roles in creating the
innovative garments featured here. Therefore, in addition
to the individuals named in the following pages we have
included houses founded by, operated by, or known for
producing designs by women.

ELIZABETH KECKLEY

Keckley was born into slavery in 1818 in Virginia. As a young girl, she was sent to work for various members of her owner's family in Virginia, North Carolina, and Missouri, suffering harsh treatment and rape that resulted in her becoming pregnant at age fourteen. By 1847 she was working for the Garland family in St. Louis. Facing financial difficulties, the Garlands became dependent on Keckley's talents as a dressmaker to rise out of debt. Her reputation for fine-quality clothing grew, and after a few years she was able to earn enough money to purchase her freedom.

In 1860 Keckley moved to Baltimore and then settled in Washington, DC, where she quickly and astutely set up shop, completing commissions for Mrs. Robert E. Lee and Mrs. Jefferson Davis. Within a year, she was recommended to Mary Todd Lincoln, who had just arrived at the capital. The two women immediately hit it off, and Keckley became the official White House modiste and confidant of Mrs. Lincoln while still maintaining her shop. In 1868 Keckley published *Behind the Scenes: or, Thirty Years a Slave and Four Years in the White House*, considered one of the most candid and poignant of narratives of an enslaved person. The book included details about the Lincoln family that, while never disputed, were considered controversial, and Keckley was forced to leave the capital. She accepted a teaching position at Wilberforce University in Ohio (the first black-owned and -operated college) and passed on her skills to a number of hopeful designers. —PS

above: Elizabeth Keckley (American, 1818–1907), about 1861

opposite: Elizabeth Keckley, dress made for Mary Todd Lincoln, about 1861, Smithsonian National Museum of American History, bequest of Mrs. Julian James, 1923, 70138

MARIA THERESA BALDWIN HOLLANDER

At a time when a married woman's property usually belonged to her husband, her labor and earnings subsumed into the household economy and often recorded under his name, Hollander charted a more independent course for her professional life. After she married Jacob L. Hollander, a New York furrier and cap maker who had emigrated from Germany, the couple and their children moved to Boston, seeking fresh opportunities after his business failed. Around 1848 she set up a business making and selling children's clothes. Records show that by 1855 Maria and Jacob Hollander had separate listings in the Boston city directory, with Maria selling children's clothing at 380 Washington Street and Jacob selling hats at 31 North Street. By the late 1860s Maria was joined in business by her oldest son, Louis. A company history notes that Maria sent one of her sons on sixty trips to Paris and London over a period of fifteen years to track the latest fashion trends and procure goods for her Boston store. Eventually, the family consolidated their separate enterprises into L. P. Hollander & Company, which grew into a major retailer in Boston and New York. The firm continued to flourish after Maria's death in 1885 under the leadership of her sons and other family members who remained involved with the business into the 1920s. —PBR

opposite and right: Maria Theresa Baldwin Hollander (American, 1812–1885), founder, L. P. Hollander & Company, Boston, dress (bodice and skirt), 1875–85, PEM, Gift of Rebecca Haskell for the Chestnut Street Associates, 1985, 136890

MARIA MONACI GALLENGA

Gallenga found inspiration in the colors, textures, and patterns of medieval and Renaissance Europe. In 1914 the award-winning artist opened a studio in Florence, where she perfected a technique for printing on fabric using carved wooden blocks and specialized in the creation of elegant stenciled and hand-painted clothing and textile panels. While several of her contemporaries were likewise exploring this aesthetic—Mariano Fortuny and his wife, Henriette Negrin, for example—Gallenga's precision and sensitivity to color resulted in especially striking creations. Treating her designs as art, Gallenga frequently worked her signature into her patterns, and her gowns became synonymous with the aesthetic of the cultural elite of the late 1910s and early 1920s.

Her work drew the attention of an international clientele, and in 1928, following her participation in the 1925 Exposition Internationale des Arts Décoratifs in Paris, she opened Boutique Italienne in that city with fellow designers Bice Pittoni and Carla Visconti di Modrone. Gallenga was an ardent promoter of Italian artisans, and her store served as a portal for Italian design until its closing in 1934. —PS

opposite and above: Maria Monaci Gallenga (Italian, 1880–1944), evening dress, 1910–20, Collection of Jimmy Raye, Salem, Massachusetts

LUCY DUFF GORDON

As the sculptor sees his dreams translated into line, and the painter sees his in terms of color, so mine were expressed in the drapery of a wisp of chiffon, or the fall of a satin fold.

A maverick in life and in fashion, Lucy Duff Gordon was a designer and entrepreneur whose innovations remain influential today. In 1893, following a divorce from her first husband, she opened Maison Lucile in London. While her designs were the essence of femininity, savvy marketing and promotional practices revealed her business acumen. She introduced "mannequin parades," precursors to today's fashion shows, that featured young women dressed in the latest styles performing with special music and lighting. Duff Gordon hired leading interior decorators to create elegant retail environments that showcased her fashions. Her fashion lines included garments, lingerie, perfumes, and accessories, an approach later adopted by Christian Dior and many of today's designers. Lucile Ltd. introduced sensuous, delicate lingerie that contrasted with the restrictive and confining corsets and bustles of the late 1800s. By 1915 Lucile Ltd. had fashion houses in London, Paris, New York, and Chicago and had become a multimillion-dollar business.

Duff Gordon's notoriety only increased in 1912 following the *Titanic*'s disastrous maiden voyage, when she and her husband, Cosmo, boarded a lifeboat with a few other first-class passengers while the majority of those on board perished. During World War I, Duff Gordon closed Lucile's Paris branch and expanded operations in New York, where she dressed stage and film stars and designed costumes for the Ziegfeld Follies theatrical revue. Counting royalty, notable beauties, and famous performers among its clients, Lucile Ltd. maintained a high profile in the press and made Duff Gordon the first female international celebrity designer. —PBR

opposite and right: Lucy Duff Gordon (British, 1863–1935), dress, 1913–15, for Lucile Ltd., PEM, Gift of Mrs. James J. Minot, 1979, 134686

GABRIELLE CHANEL

Fashion passes; style remains.

Throughout her career, Chanel created fashion that liberated women to pursue modern, active lifestyles. She learned to sew in an orphanage run by nuns, where Chanel was educated after the death of her mother. She began her fashion career as a milliner in 1910, opened a couture house in Paris in 1912, and soon added shops in the seaside resorts of Deauville and Biarritz with financial backing provided by wealthy male lovers. Her early work featured dresses and garments made of wool jersey, a stretchy, utilitarian fabric typically used for men's undergarments, not for fashionable clothes. She closed her establishments in 1914 with the onset of World War I.

Reopening her businesses in 1919, Chanel designed simple, practical clothing with styles pared to essentials, to be worn in a relaxed manner that defined modernity. She drew inspiration from sportswear for tennis, swimming, and golf for her daytime designs and borrowed elements of menswear for her androgynous, tailored suits that appealed to young women entering the workforce—and to wealthy clients intrigued by youthful styles that suggested an aura of "deluxe poverty." In the 1920s, Chanel's short, slim, and shimmering evening dresses were the essence of Parisian chic. —PBR

left: Gabrielle Chanel (French, 1883–1971), evening dress, 1939, for Chanel, Kunstmuseum Den Haag, 1003192

opposite left: Gabrielle Chanel, evening dress, about 1925, for Chanel, Kunstmuseum Den Haag, 1023330

opposite right: Model in a dress by Gabrielle Chanel, 1926, for Chanel, photo by Edward Steichen

Chanel was among the first designers to exploit the "power of personality," using her social connections with artists, investors, and patrons to build her brand. In 1939, as World War II began, Chanel closed her fashion house and later fled to Switzerland following an affair with a Nazi officer during the German occupation of Paris. In 1954 she returned to France and presented her first collection of the postwar era. It countered Christian Dior's so-called New Look, which had debuted in 1947 and which Chanel felt returned women to confining, structured, voluminous garments of the prewar era. Her collection featured tweed suits with jackets trimmed with braid and knee-length skirts worn with soft blouses and accessorized with pearl necklaces, chain belts, and two-toned sling-back pumps. This look epitomized her fashion empire's legendary style—one that would be reinterpreted after Chanel's death by creative director Karl Lagerfeld and his successor, Virginie Viard, appointed in 2019. —PBR

left: Gabrielle Chanel, afternoon dress, about 1960–62, for Chanel, Kunstmuseum Den Haag, 1003193

opposite: Gabrielle Chanel, suit, 1966, for Chanel, Kunstmuseum Den Haag, 0783060

JEANNE PAQUIN / CALLOT SOEURS

Although once overshadowed by male couturiers Charles Frederick Worth and Paul Poiret, Jeanne Paquin emerged in recent scholarship as a major force in fashion of the late nineteenth and early twentieth centuries. The daughter of a physician, Paquin found employment managing the atelier of Maggy Rouff (pp. 57–59). In 1891 she opened, in partnership with her husband, the House of Paquin and became the first major female couturiere in Paris. The house quickly expanded and eventually employed 2,700 people. She blended tailoring, dressmaking, and drapery in exquisitely designed and constructed garments with details that added comfort and practicality. Her designs spanned day to evening wear in response to changing lifestyles, and she was attentive to the needs of clients that included European royalty, aristocrats, socialites, and courtesans. In 1900 Paquin was asked to organize the fashion section at the Exposition Universelle in Paris. In 1913 she received the Légion d'honneur, becoming the first female designer to receive that prestigious accolade from the French government. In 1917 the Chambre Syndicale de la Haute Couture, the organization that oversees couture designers of Paris, appointed Paquin its first female president.

Other female-led couture houses soon followed. In 1895 the four Callot sisters—Marie, Marthe, Régine, and Joséphine, the daughters of a lacemaker and an artist—founded the fashion house of Callot Soeurs. It was renowned for the artistry and superb craftsmanship of its designs. Like Lucile Ltd. and Jenny (pp. 36–37 and 46–47), Callot Soeurs cultivated an extensive clientele in the United States. Early in her career, Madeleine Vionnet (pp. 48–49) worked for Callot Soeurs as the head of the atelier and credited the sisters' influence on her later work. —PBR

left: Evening dress, about 1920–24, for Callot Soeurs (French, active 1895–1937), Kunstmuseum Den Haag, 322376

opposite left: Evening dress, about 1925, for Callot Soeurs, Kunstmuseum Den Haag, 1022537

opposite right: Jeanne Paquin (French, 1896–1936), dress, 1921, Kunstmuseum Den Haag, 0322364

MIES VAN OS

opposite and left: Mies van Os (Dutch, 1901–1982), walking ensemble, about 1925–26, Kunstmuseum Den Haag, 0241593

above: Mies van Os, dress, about 1925–26, Kunstmuseum Den Haag, 810855

JEANNE ADÈLE BERNARD SACERDOTE

Although little known today, the Paris fashion house Jenny—founded by Jeanne Adèle Bernard Sacerdote (whose nickname was Jenny)—created garments embodying new freedoms for women in the early twentieth century and captured the spirit of the Jazz Age. Sacerdote established the firm in 1909 in partnership with dressmaker Marie Le Corre. Sacerdote served as creative director, while Le Corre managed a team of seamstresses and technicians. Jenny soon gained a reputation for dresses and suits characterized by simplicity of form and line, exceptional materials, and distinctive details that set the firm apart from competitors. In 1914 Jenny moved to a new building on the Champs-Élysées designed and built specifically for dressmaking. A year later Jenny exhibited its designs at the Panama-Pacific International Exposition in San Francisco and promoted its fashions to American consumers, who soon became an important part of the firm's clientele.

Jenny drew inspiration from sporting and athletic clothes, with simple columnar forms and narrow skirts that promoted freedom of movement. It is credited with popularizing the bateau, or boat, neckline. In 1925 Jenny exhibited its works at the Exposition Internationale des Arts Décoratifs in Paris, an event that defined Art Deco. The firm's youthful garments in simple shapes were a canvas for artistic surface ornamentation, boldly patterned fabrics, and beadwork in the newly popular style. In 1928 Sacerdote won the prestigious Grand Prix de Paris d'Élégance award, given at what was considered the outstanding fashion event of the season. The Depression in the United States precipitated the decline of the house of Jenny during the 1930s, as the firm's American clients could no longer afford imported French fashions. —PBR

right and opposite: Jeanne Adèle Bernard Sacerdote (French, 1868–1962), dress, 1927, for Jenny, PEM, Gift of Mrs. Edward Gates, 1970, 132306

MADELEINE VIONNET

I don't know what fashion is. I make clothes I believe in.

Madeleine Vionnet's pioneering experiments with the drape and movement of fabric set the tone for fashion in the twentieth century. Often referred to as an "architect among dressmakers," Vionnet established an enduring new model for the relationship between dress and the female body. She began her career under the English court dressmaker Kate Reilly and later refined her tailoring skills with French couturieres Callot Soeurs (pp. 42–43) and Jacques Doucet. By the time she opened her first atelier in 1912, Vionnet had become a masterful designer and a technically rigorous seamstress. She had also developed an interest in freeing the female form from the highly structured, corseted garments of the previous decades.

In the 1920s Vionnet famously perfected the bias cut, a method of cutting a textile diagonally across the grain. This technique allowed fabric to drape across the body and move with the wearer, creating an elegant silhouette reminiscent of ancient Grecian costume. Vionnet's sensuous designs rendered in luxurious fabrics were suggestive of the bodily landscape beneath, instantly shifting the expected silhouette for women's evening wear. Those designs became a hallmark of Vionnet's oeuvre and a staple of the aesthetic of early Hollywood. Though Vionnet is less well known today than some of her peers, her artistry remains an influence on fashion, as designers continue to mimic her construction methods in clothing that celebrates the female body. —LM

opposite: Models in gowns by Madeleine Vionnet (French, 1876–1975) for *Vogue*, 1930, photo by Edward Steichen

right: Madeleine Vionnet, evening dress, about 1930–31, Kunstmuseum Den Haag, 0393991

MADAME GRÈS / JEANNE LANVIN

Madame Grès—born Germaine Émilie Krebs and known early in her career as Alix Barton—opened her first couture house in 1932. Her early interest in sculpture had been discouraged by her family, so she turned to millinery and dressmaking— though traces of her artistic training remain in the Greco-Roman character of her classically draped designs. During her career, Grès made forays into designs inspired by saris, kimono, and serapes, and produced skillfully tailored women's suits, but her focus remained chiefly on couture gowns. Her intricate yet minimalist draping technique and respect for the female body influenced later designers such as Azzedine Alaïa. Grès's designs were worn by numerous mid-twentieth-century celebrities, including Wallis Simpson, Paloma Picasso, Grace Kelly, Marlene Dietrich, and Greta Garbo. Grès was the first living designer to be the subject of a solo exhibition at the Metropolitan Museum of Art.

Jeanne Lanvin opened her first millinery shop in Paris in 1889 and four years later established Lanvin (Mademoiselle Jeanne) Modes. The elegant wardrobe she designed for her daughter ignited such interest that she opened a children's clothing department in 1908. Soon these orders exceeded those for hats, and Lanvin opened a women's department. Her beaded and embroidered creations contrasted with the sportier designs of contemporaries such as Chanel (pp. 38–41). Offering day and evening clothes, lingerie, and outerwear, Lanvin expanded her business to include furs, sportswear, home décor, and perfume—her Arpège fragrance achieved legendary status. She found success in America following a display of French couture at the 1915 Panama–Pacific International Exposition in San Francisco. Through the 1920s her business grew to include twenty-three ateliers employing 800 people. Lanvin established an empire that, while no longer offering couture, stands as the oldest fashion house in Paris. —PS

right and opposite: Madame Grès (Alix Barton; French, 1903–1993), evening dress, about 1933–34, Kunstmuseum Den Haag, 1003180

left: Jeanne Lanvin (French, 1867–1946), afternoon dress, 1930, Kunstmuseum Den Haag, 0322361

above: Jeanne Lanvin, evening dress, about 1930–31, Kunstmuseum Den Haag, 0555942

above: Jeanne Lanvin, ensemble, 1930, Kunstmuseum Den Haag, 1025652

right: Jeanne Lanvin, evening dress, 1930, Kunstmuseum Den Haag, 0555943

ADELE SIMPSON

I don't make clothes for a woman to make an entrance in. She has to live in them.

Simpson was born in New York City, the fifth daughter of Latvian immigrants. In 1924, after completing studies at Pratt Institute, she secured the position of head designer at Seventh Avenue outlet Ben Girshel, and then later at Mary Lee. After designing under her own name, she bought Mary Lee and renamed it Adele Simpson, which she helmed for four successful decades. Best known for her stylish, comfortable clothing, Simpson specialized in what she called "realistic" fashions. She promoted the use of coordinating separates that could take a wearer from day to night, which became a favorite of active working women everywhere. Long before the cotton T-shirt became ubiquitous, Simpson was known as the designer who "took cotton out of the kitchen." In 1953 she was named winner of the Cotton Council's Cotton Fashion Award for her innovative use of the fabric in cocktail dresses—a development that helped pave the way for the material to become a twenty-first-century fashion staple. —PS

opposite: Model Beverly Johnson in an ensemble by Adele Simpson (American, 1904–1995) with Van Cleef & Arpels diamond accessories for *Vogue*, 1974

right: Adele Simpson, dress, about 1947–53, Kunstmuseum Den Haag, 0321922

LUCILLE MANGUIN / MARGARÈT

left: Lucille Manguin (French, active 1928–1960), dress, 1951, Kunstmuseum Den Haag, 0322235

above: Dress, 1951, for Margarèt (French, active 20th century), Kunstmuseum Den Haag, 0322068

MAGGY ROUFF

Born Marguerite Besançon de Wagner to fashion designer parents who operated the Paris branch of the Viennese House of Drécoll, Rouff opened her own fashion house in 1929. She initially produced understated sportswear but later became known for her harmonious use of feminine details such as ruffles, shirring, and bias cuts. During the 1930s Rouff was head of the Association pour la Protection des Industries Artistiques Saisonnières (Association of Seasonal Art Industries), an important antipiracy and counterfeiting trade network of dressmakers, suppliers, and representatives of related industries, founded by Madeleine Vionnet (see pp. 48–49) in 1921. Rouff's customers were drawn to her elegant designs that combined novelty and taste to chic effect. Rouff's daughter, Anne-Marie Besançon de Wagner, took over the house after Rouff's retirement in 1948 but, unable to attract a younger clientele, closed the establishment in 1965. —PS

above: A model in a houndstooth ensemble by Maggy Rouff (French, 1896–1971), Paris, 1955

opposite: Maggy Rouff, "College" coat, 1949, Kunstmuseum Den Haag, 0322076

above: Maggy Rouff, "Lucerne" dress, 1949, Kunstmuseum Den Haag, 0321925

right: Maggy Rouff, "Bénares" evening dress, 1937, Kunstmuseum Den Haag, 1022538

HATTIE CARNEGIE / SALLY MILGRIM

American designers Hattie Carnegie and Sally Milgrim left their stamp on fashion during the decades after the Great Depression. Born in Vienna, Henrietta Kanengeiser emigrated with her family to New York in 1892 and settled on the Lower East Side. By 1909 she had changed her name to Carnegie (after the wealthiest man in America) and founded a custom clothing and millinery shop. In 1923 she moved the business to a town house in Midtown Manhattan and offered garments, accessories, jewelry, lingerie, and perfume. As Carnegie could not sew or draft patterns herself, she hired talented young designers such as Norman Norell, Claire McCardell (p. 74), and James Galanos, all of whom later founded their own firms. Fashion magazines promoted the Carnegie look, featuring structured, perfectly fitted suits and dresses with simple, elegant details. Her high-profile clientele included film stars and socialites such as Wallis Simpson. Carnegie received the Coty American Fashion Critics' Award in 1948 for her role in advancing American fashion.

Born in New York, Milgrim was the daughter of Austrian immigrants. At a young age she married Charles Milgrim, a partner in a custom suit business on the Lower East Side, and she soon became the company's designer. In the 1920s the firm moved uptown to a fashionable address on Fifty-Seventh Street near Fifth Avenue, offering custom and ready-to-wear garments, including evening gowns. Milgrim opened stores in Midwestern cities and Florida and created the Salymil label, a wholesale line sold to retailers around the country. Eleanor Roosevelt chose Milgrim to design a custom gown to wear at her husband's 1933 inaugural ball, giving the designer national and international recognition. —PBR

left: Hattie Carnegie (American, b. Austria, 1889–1956), evening gown, 1930s, Collection of Jimmy Raye, Salem, Massachusetts

opposite: Sally Milgrim (American, 1891–1994), evening dress, early 1930s, PEM, Gift of Mrs. Udell S. R. White in memory of her great-grandmother, Ada Fulwiler Whitehill (1828–1912), 1973, 133358

VALENTINA

left: Valentina (Valentina Nikolaevna Sanina Schlee; American, b. Russia, 1899–1989), evening dress, 1930s, Museum of Fine Arts, Boston, Museum purchase with funds donated by the Fashion Council, Museum of Fine Arts, Boston, 2011.2057

above: Valentina in a dress of her own design, 1940

ELIZABETH HAWES

Hawes was a journalist, writer, feminist, union organizer, and one of the most influential American fashion designers of the early twentieth century. From a young age, she was fastidious about style. She made her own clothes and sold her first collection to a Philadelphia store at age twelve. After studying economics at Vassar College, she moved to Paris in 1925 to become a couturiere. Instead she ended up working for a firm as a "copy pirate," lifting styles from French designers like Chanel and Vionnet (pp. 38–41 and 48–49). After leaving that disreputable role and a stint with couturiere Nicole Groult, Hawes returned to the United States and in 1928 opened her own studio. Crediting the man who was briefly her husband (a sculptor she met in Paris) with helping her to see clothes as architecture, Hawes proceeded to rethink womenswear by ignoring Parisian styles and advocating comfort achieved through exquisite cut—and in the process unknowingly laid the foundation for what became known as the American Look. In 1931 Hawes became the first American to display her collection in Paris: twelve ensembles "created for American women, out of American materials, inspired by American background." When in 1932 Dorothy Shaver, president of Lord & Taylor, began her pioneering effort to promote American designers by name, her first call was to Hawes. Hawes went on to become an outspoken critic of the fashion industry and a champion of ready-to-wear styles. *Fashion Is Spinach*, her witty insider's critique of the fashion industry of the 1920s and 1930s, is the most memorable of her many books. —PS

right: Elizabeth Hawes (American, 1903–1971), evening dress, about 1934, Museum of Fine Arts, Boston, Gift of Mrs. Frederick W. Hilles, 53.418

ELSA SCHIAPARELLI

Schiaparelli is above all the dressmaker of eccentricity. Jean Cocteau

Many consider Schiaparelli to be one of the most influential designers between the World Wars, along with her great rival Gabrielle Chanel (pp. 38–41). Schiaparelli was born in Rome; her mother was from an aristocratic family, and her father was a scholar and library director. After a brief marriage in the early 1920s, Schiaparelli was introduced to an artistic circle in Paris that included Francis Picabia, Man Ray, and Marcel Duchamp. With few resources and a young daughter to support, Schiaparelli designed a gown for her friend Gabrielle Picabia that caught the eye of the leading French designer Paul Poiret, who became a friend and supporter. By the late 1920s Schiaparelli had produced knitwear and sportswear with designs inspired by Cubism, Art Deco, and Surrealism. She collaborated with major avant-garde figures such as Salvador Dalí (a lobster evening dress worn by Wallis Simpson) and Jean Cocteau (a jacket with embroidery by Lesage based on a sketch by the artist).

In 1935 Schiaparelli opened the Schiap Boutique in Paris, where she created and sold some of her most imaginative works, including the Circus collection of 1938, in which runway fashion became theatrical spectacle. In 1940 Schiaparelli left Paris for New York. After the war, she returned to Paris and produced collections into the early 1950s but was unable to adapt to changes in taste and closed her couture house in 1954. —PBR

left: Elsa Schiaparelli (Italian, 1890–1973), dress from the Circus collection, 1938, Kunstmuseum Den Haag, 1058927

opposite: Model in a dress designed by Elsa Schiaparelli, 1947

DAHAVA KREISBERG-KROCHMAL / NINA RICCI / MARIE-LOUISE CARVEN

I decided to make haute couture outfits in my size because I was too short to wear the creations of the top couturiers, who only ever showed their designs on towering girls. Marie-Louise Carven

left: Dahava Kreisberg-Krochmal (Dutch, b. Austria, 1915–1997) with Anna Nightingale-Krochmal (Dutch, 1923–2016), dress, about 1959, for Jolo Couture, Kunstmuseum Den Haag, 1002162

above: Nina Ricci (French, b. Italy, 1883–1970), coat, about 1965, Kunstmuseum Den Haag, 1002431

opposite: Marie-Louise Carven (French, 1909–2015), dress, about 1946–47, for House of Carven, Kunstmuseum Den Haag, 055623

ANN LOWE

I love my clothes, and I'm particular about who wears them.

Known as "society's best-kept secret" and one of the first prominent black designers, Lowe was born in Clayton, Alabama, to a seamstress who served Montgomery's elite. She exhibited exceptional talent early on: using scraps from her mother's commissions, Lowe began fashioning tiny fabric flowers—a skill that became one of her hallmarks. Lowe jump-started her career when she was sixteen years old by finishing four commissions for the first family of Alabama after her mother's untimely death in 1914. Three years later, she took her young son to New York and studied couture at S. T. Taylor Design School. Due to segregation, the school insisted she work in isolation; nevertheless, Lowe produced exemplary work and graduated early. In 1919 Lowe set up shop in Florida, designing custom gowns and became a smash success.

In 1928 Lowe moved back to New York, designing for Henri Bendel, Hattie Carnegie (p. 60), and Saks Fifth Avenue and serving as a fashion correspondent for the *New York Age*. After Olivia de Havilland chose one of Lowe's designs to wear to the 1947 Academy Awards (where she won the best actress Oscar), the designer opened her own shop, landing a coveted spot on Madison Avenue in 1950. Lowe's client list is a who's who of the social register. The Rockefellers, the Posts, and three generations of Auchinclosses regularly sought her out, but her most famous client was Jacqueline Bouvier, who wore a custom Ann Lowe wedding dress to marry John F. Kennedy in 1953. —PS

right: Ann Lowe (American, 1898–1981), dress, 1966–67, Collection of the Smithsonian National Museum of African American History and Culture, Gift of the Black Fashion Museum founded by Lois K. Alexander-Lane, 2007.3.19

TINA LESER

Successful design always reflects purpose.

Leser's imaginative approach to sportswear introduced an era of unfussy dressing for American women during and after World War II. She eschewed the formality of couture, believing that women desired clothing that was "amusing and interesting" rather than highly tailored and accessorized. While her designs were lauded for being unexpected and new, Leser maintained that her main goal was to create garments that were wearable and, above all else, fun.

Leser traveled extensively and lived for periods in both Hawaii and India, and her clothing—particularly her resort and leisurewear—took inspiration from the many cultures she encountered abroad. Borrowing elements of non-Western textiles and costumes, she fluidly mixed them with recognizable American forms. Her takes on foreign dress included such items as Spanish toreador pants, Indian sari-inspired dresses, and a reworking of the Hawaiian sarong. Taken out of their original context, these designs felt fresh and novel to an American audience grounded by experiences of the Depression and war. Leser was also conscious to build partnerships with the international artisans she commissioned to produce her textiles. She helped them to license their patterns, ensuring they would receive fair compensation for their contributions. —LM

right: Tina Leser (American, 1910–1986), dress, 1950s, PEM, museum purchase, 2019.21.1

ROSE MARIE REID /
CAROLYN SCHNURER

Along with Tina Leser, Rose Marie Reid and Carolyn Schnurer were instrumental in evolving swimwear styles from the saggy, itchy wool tunics of the early 1900s into functional, fashionable sportswear designed for active, stylish women. The trio also created a range of beautiful, practical resort wear that helped define the emerging American Look of the mid-twentieth century. Reid in particular worked hard to ensure that the fit, comfort, and functionality of her athletic swimwear maintained a sense of glamour. Her infrastructure, underwiring, boning, and other techniques are still used in lingerie and swimwear development today. Schnurer and Leser focused on creating a range of suits that could be adjusted and adapted to a wide range of body types, looking to cotton as their material of choice. The swimwear of these designers frequently appeared in magazines such as *Vogue*, *Harper's Bazaar*, and *Life*, and with them, fashion editorials began to adopt a new style of playful fashion photography. Each designer was an excellent entrepreneur and shrewd innovator who went on to receive numerous accolades. —PS

right: Tina Leser, swimsuit, late 1950s; Rose Marie Reid (American, 1908–1978), swimsuit, about 1962; Carolyn Schnurer (American, 1908–1978), swimsuit, early to mid-1950s, Collection of Jimmy Raye, Salem, Massachusetts

BONNIE CASHIN

To function in a complicated world calls for uncomplicated clothes.

Although not a household name today, Cashin was among the most groundbreaking American fashion designers of the twentieth century. Raised in California, she began her career designing costumes for the film industry, theater, and ballet. In the early 1930s the Roxy Theater in New York City hired Cashin to design stage costumes for a showgirl troupe called the Roxyettes. In the early 1940s she returned to California, where she designed costumes for films produced by 20th Century Fox, including *Laura* (1944) and *Anna and the King of Siam* (1946).

During World War II, Cashin joined Vera Maxwell and Claire McCardell (p. 74) on a committee appointed to design women's civil defense uniforms. Her experience with the military had a lasting impact on her work in promoting freedom of movement, comfort, protection, simplicity, and practicality. In 1952 she opened Bonnie Cashin Designs and freelanced for several companies, including Sills & Co. and Coach. She became known for layered ensembles that were well suited for travel and active lifestyles, and loose-fitting outerwear such as coats, capes, and ponchos. An avid traveler, Cashin drew inspiration from Asian garments such as the kimono and the panung, a wrapped garment from Thailand, adapting them for contemporary fashion. Cashin received numerous awards during her career and was inducted into the Coty American Fashion Critics' Hall of Fame in 1972. The Cashin Archive maintains a social media account, @cashincopy, which documents the influence of Cashin's classic designs on today's fashion. —PBR

right: Bonnie Cashin (American, 1915–2000), coatdress, about 1967, for Sills & Co., PEM, Gift of Susanna B. Weld, 2000, 138030

opposite: Bonnie Cashin, handbag, 1960s, for Coach, PEM, Gift of Laura Kramer in memory of Lee Kramer, 2015.9.48

FROM THE
COACH
COLLECTION OF
"CASHIN CARRY"
BAGS AND ACCESSO-
RIES DESIGNED BY
BONNIE CASHIN

CLAIRE McCARDELL

I've always wondered why women's clothes had to be delicate—why they couldn't be practical and sturdy as well as feminine.

American designers of the mid-twentieth century began to challenge the global dominance of French couture with a new approach: designer sportswear. Although French designers Gabrielle Chanel (pp. 38–41) and Jean Patou had adapted elements of sporting clothes in their day dresses and knitwear in the 1920s, American designers established designer sportswear as a major category for custom and ready-to-wear fashion. Although several designers contributed to this movement, McCardell stands out for her groundbreaking work in creating fashion attuned to changes in women's lives that demanded elegant, well-cut, and practical clothes.

In 1928 McCardell graduated from the New York School of Fine and Applied Arts (now known as Parsons School of Design) and later found employment with Townley Frocks, a New York clothing manufacturer. Among her innovations were the Monastic, a loose, unstructured dress that conformed to the wearer's body with a belt, and the Popover, a wrapped garment with a large pocket sold as a stylish utility dress. She also designed cotton bathing suits, playsuits, and travel clothes that offered comfort and ease of movement. McCardell's garments were characterized by their use of pleating and draping, precise cuts, hardware fasteners, ties and belts, pockets, and other no-nonsense features. She favored practical fabrics such as cotton shirting, denim, and wool jersey in rich colors and patterns. In 1955 *Time* magazine featured McCardell in a cover article, and in 1990 *Life* magazine listed her as one of the hundred most important Americans of the twentieth century. —PBR

right: Claire McCardell (American, 1905–1958), dress, 1940–60, for Townley Frocks Inc., PEM, The Albert Szabo and Brenda Dyer Szabo Collection, 2018.29.3

PAULINE TRIGÈRE

Fashion is what they say you should do, and style is what you do for yourself.

For fifty years, Trigère created women's clothing marked by sophisticated tailoring, impeccably clean lines, and innovative ideas. Designing with the careful eye of a Parisian couturiere, Trigère translated her immaculate tailoring skills for an American audience. She launched her business in the 1940s with her brother Robert, presenting crisply tailored suits, A-line dresses, and reversible outwear. She continued with such imaginative contributions as the use of unconventional fabrics like wool and cotton in evening wear. She soon elevated the jumpsuit to high fashion and in 1967 introduced a rhinestone bra top that would routinely be revived over the following decades. As Trigère's designs evolved, her adherence to complex construction and clean lines lent her clothing an enduring air of elegance and timeless appeal.

Active until her death at age ninety-three, Trigère was known in both fashion and life as an uncompromising force. Her toughness was born of necessity: she left Paris in 1937 as the Nazi threat increased and began her business in New York as a single mother. She recalled, "I never set my goals to become a great designer. I just had to make money to live." Even as her business grew, she maintained tight control over its every aspect and held firmly to her standards. That tenacity was evident in 1961 when she became the first name designer to employ a black model, never wavering from her decision amid racist threats. —LM

left: Pauline Trigère (American, b. France, 1908–2002) takes the stage at a 1992 fashion show

above: Pauline Trigère, suit (jacket and dress), 1960s, Collection of Jimmy Raye, Salem, Massachusetts

FAIZE KUHAR /
SEVIM BABAN

Great fashion and great designers are not limited to Paris, London, Milan, New York, Los Angeles, and Tokyo. The Turkish fashion house of Faize-Sevim has produced elegant ensembles in Istanbul and Ankara since the mid-1950s. Run by the sisters Faize Kuhar and Sevim Baban along with Sevim's daughter, Alev Esen, the firm specializes in custom evening and event dresses and wedding attire for prominent Turkish clients that include actresses, performers, socialites, and wives of government officials. It has also attracted Saudi Arabian clients, including members of the Saudi royal family. Noted for the lavish handwork of its creations, Faize-Sevim uses luxury fabrics, sequins, and other materials from Paris as well as high-quality textiles sourced locally. At the height of the firm's popularity, Faize-Sevim engaged forty-two embroiderers and upwards of 350 employees. The firm is credited with hosting the first public fashion runway show held in Turkey and employed the country's first professional fashion model, Lale Belkıs, who went on to model for international brands such as Christian Dior and Saks Fifth Avenue. With its founders now in their eighties and nineties, the firm produces work in smaller quantities, but it is still accepting commissions from select clients. —PBR

opposite and left: Faize Kuhar (Turkish, b. 1927) and Sevim Baban (Turkish, b. 1933), evening dress, 1960s, for Faize-Sevim, Adnan Ege Kutay Collection

MARY QUANT

It wasn't me or Courrèges who invented the miniskirt anyway—it was the girls in the street who did it.

Long touted as the inventor of the miniskirt, Quant is much more than a raised hemline. Born in London, she opened her boutique, Bazaar, in 1955 on the ground floor of the home she shared with her husband on the King's Road in Chelsea. The self-taught Quant rejected the highly structured styles and techniques of high-end couturiers, relying on her eye and her sensitivity to an evolving generation coming out of postwar England. Her alteration of popular patterns allowed for the birth of the shift dress and the miniskirt, both of which were made famous by supermodel Twiggy and adored by bohemians and the trendsetting Chelsea Set alike.

Quant's clothes championed evolution, liberation, revolution, and female independence. Using bold colors, odd materials (she used PVC for both tunics and shoes), and redesigned shapes, she worked to revitalize a world struggling to move forward. Her innovations didn't end with the miniskirt: one of the first celebrity designers, she was her own best model; she built a cosmetics empire that streamlined everyday cosmetic application; and licensing her name allowed for total penetration into the consumer market. It is estimated that by the end of the 1960s close to 7 million women had a Mary Quant product in their homes. Her designs proved to be a major foundation for the Swinging Sixties, and to this day they look like they just walked off the runway. —PS

right: Mary Quant (British, b. 1936), dress, about 1965–66, Kunstmuseum Den Haag, 0634503

opposite: Model in an oilskin outfit by Mary Quant, London, 1963

EMMY VAN LEERSUM / MARIANNE DAVID / ALICE EDELING

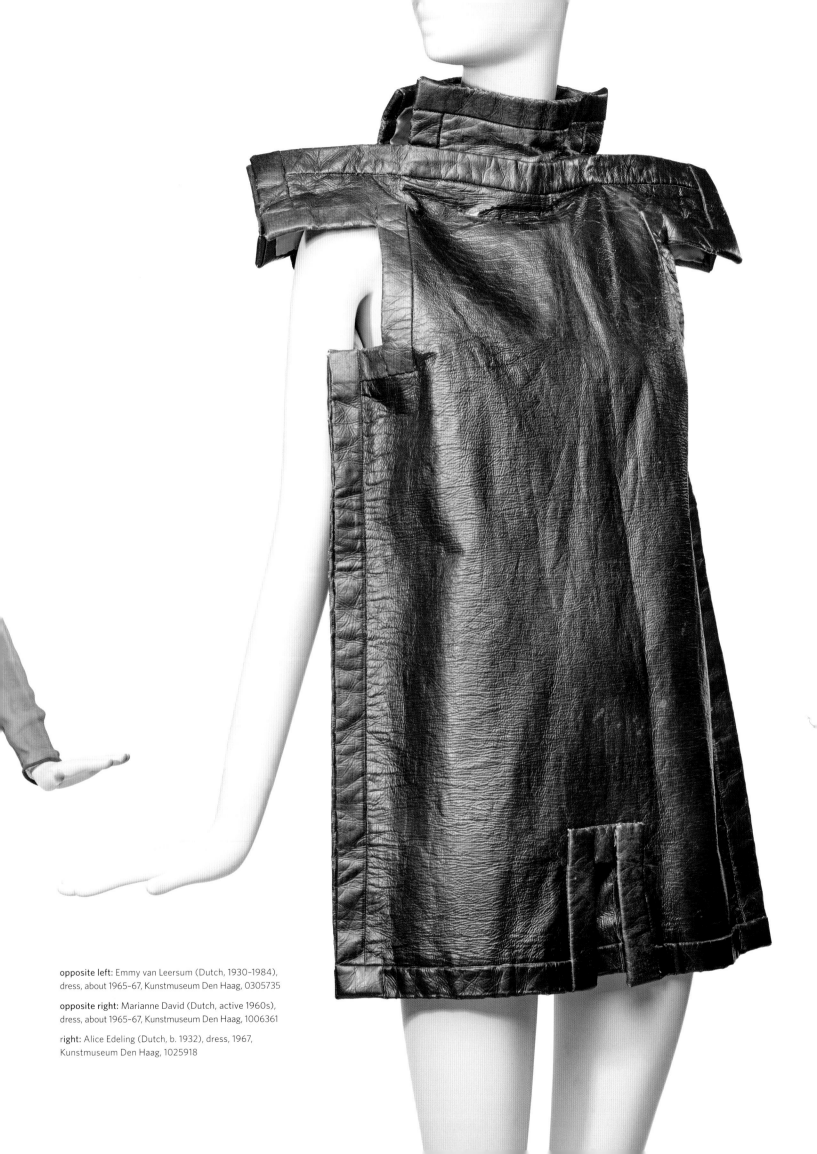

opposite left: Emmy van Leersum (Dutch, 1930–1984),
dress, about 1965–67, Kunstmuseum Den Haag, 0305735

opposite right: Marianne David (Dutch, active 1960s),
dress, about 1965–67, Kunstmuseum Den Haag, 1006361

right: Alice Edeling (Dutch, b. 1932), dress, 1967,
Kunstmuseum Den Haag, 1025918

ARMI RATIA / VUOKKO ESKOLIN-NURMESNIEMI

Finnish design firm Marimekko, founded in 1951 by Armi Ratia and her husband, Viljo, created boldly modern clothes and printed textiles that stand at the apex of mid-century Modernist expression. Marimekko evolved out of the couple's first company, Printex, that produced cotton textiles in abstract patterns, screen printed by hand using high-quality dyes and distinctive color palettes. To expand sales, Ratia produced an experimental line of clothing under the name Marimekko, which translates as "little dress for Mary." Ads showed models in active stances in the Finnish landscape wearing bold, comfortable garments that suggested freedom and individuality. The company soon attracted a following that included artists, intellectuals, and creative individuals who valued Modernist ideals and aesthetics. Architects and designers favored Marimekko textiles, and the company expanded into an integrated lifestyle brand combining fashion and interior design. Although trained in design, Ratia earned recognition as a pioneering female executive in the male-dominated corporate manufacturing field.

Marimekko hired talented artists such as Vuokko Eskolin-Nurmesniemi and Annika Rimala, who created simple, loose, and unrestrictive clothing in contrast to prevailing styles of the 1950s that emphasized form-fitting, confining, and structured garments. In the late 1950s Eskolin-Nurmesniemi contributed to an exhibition of Finnish art and culture at Design Research in Cambridge, Massachusetts, introducing Marimekko textiles and fashion to American audiences. Jacqueline Kennedy bought several Marimekko dresses, further promoting the company's products. After leaving Marimekko in 1960, Eskolin-Nurmesniemi founded the design studio Vuokko Oy, which produced innovative textiles and clothing. Rimala worked as chief fashion designer for Marimekko from 1960 to 1982, creating printed textiles and clothing designs. —PBR

right: Vuokko Eskolin-Nurmesniemi (Finnish, b. 1930), dress, 1960s, PEM, Gift of Mrs. Christopher Weld in memory of Mrs. Kenyon Boocock, 2016.61.9; Marimekko for Design Research, dress, 1960s, PEM, Gift of Madelon C. Z. Bures, 2018.57.12; attributed to Annika Rimala (Finnish, 1936–2014) for Marimekko for Design Research, dress, 1965 PEM, Gift of Madelon C. Z. Bures, 2018.57.12

DIANE VON FÜRSTENBERG

My definition of beauty is strength and personality.

Diane von Fürstenberg, fashion powerhouse and stalwart of female empowerment, built her brand on bold, easy-to-wear clothing for the modern, self-assured woman. In 1974 Fürstenberg created a garment that would seal her status as a fashion icon and industry mogul: the wrap dress. Constructed of form-fitting jersey and available in a dizzying array of colors and patterns, the timeless, flattering design felt equally at home in the office or a nightclub. Likening the dress to traditional, single-garment costumes such as the toga or kimono, Fürstenberg noted that what set it apart was the use of jersey, a clinging fabric that intrinsically adapts itself to the wearer's form. This flexibility and ease catapulted the dress into a symbol for women's liberation and has to this day remained a staple in women's wardrobes. Fürstenberg insists the intent behind the wrap dress was to inspire self-assurance: "It is about freedom and power and confidence . . . It is really all about empowering women, and I hope that is my legacy." —LM

right: Diane von Fürstenberg (Belgian, b. 1946), wrap dress, 1975, Adnan Ege Kutay Collection

opposite: Diane von Fürstenberg in her own dress at a screening of Andy Warhol's film *Flesh for Frankenstein*, New York, 1974

SONIA RYKIEL

Everything I do is really an expression of myself, through colors and shapes. . . . At the same time, I try to explain what I feel not only as a creator but also as a woman. I cannot separate one from the other.

opposite: Model in an ensemble by Sonia Rykiel (French, 1930–2016) at Paris Fashion Week, 2008

left: Model in a 2008 Sonia Rykiel show

above: Sonia Rykiel, pantsuit, 1972, for Henri Bendel, Adnan Ege Kutay Collection

FRANKIE WELCH

Welch, who self-identifies as having Cherokee heritage, was born Mary Frances Barnett in Rome, Georgia. A great admirer of Frank Lloyd Wright, she initially wanted to study with him at the University of Wisconsin but was told the architect wouldn't accept female students. Welch's husband's job took their young family to Alexandria, Virginia, after which she settled into several years of teaching home economics. During this time she also served as a personal style consultant, which led her to open her own clothing shop in 1963.

Through her Alexandria storefront, Welch designed clothing and accessories that were coveted by women in the social and political elite. Her hallmarks, however, were scarves featuring iconic political and historical themes. They promoted various bipartisan campaigns and featured such quintessential images as trains, monuments, national emblems, and, in perhaps Welch's most recognizable work, the Cherokee alphabet. Welch went on to become a favorite designer of Betty Ford, and her work is included in the First Ladies Collection in the National Museum of American History. —PS

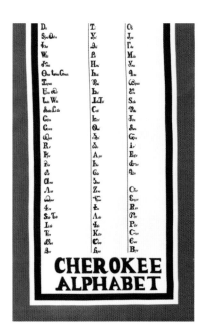

above: Frankie Welch (Cherokee heritage, b. 1924), scarf, PEM, Gift of Karen Kramer, 2015.11.3

right: Frankie Welch, dress, early to mid-1970s, PEM, Gift of Karen Kramer, 2019.65.1

ALICE POLLOCK

right: Alice Pollock (British, b. 1942), ensemble, about 1975,
Kunstmuseum Den Haag, 0634570

JACQUELINE JACOBSON

Dorothée Bis, the quintessential Paris ready-to-wear house, aims at the young swinging crowd who prefer to change their style every season if not oftener.
Bernardine Morris, *New York Times*

opposite: Jacqueline Jacobson (French, b. 1928), sweater, about 1976, for Dorothée Bis,
PEM, Gift of Petra Slinkard in memory of Carli Slinkard, 2019.65.2

LAURA ASHLEY

I don't like ephemeral things;
I like things that last forever.

above: Laura Ashley ad campaign, 1993

right: Laura Ashley (British, 1926–1985), ensemble, about 1975, Kunstmuseum Den Haag, 0242212

LILY HENKET-CONEMANS

left: Lily Henket-Conemans (Dutch, b. 1943), dress, about 1975–79, Kunstmuseum Den Haag, 394493

ZANDRA RHODES

Color gives confidence. It makes a strong statement. Here I am. Love me or hate me.

Rhodes is a luminary of London's fashion scene, creating unique and imaginative designs for the past fifty years. Trained as an artist and printmaker, she began her career producing screen-printed textiles by hand and soon branched out to designing dresses that maximized the impact of her distinctive fabrics. Rhodes produced her first collection in 1969 during fashion's transition from the mod styles of London's Swinging Sixties to the bohemian- and hippie-inspired dress of the early 1970s. Her diaphanous, colorful printed silks and chiffons were perfect for the long, romantic styles of the early 1970s. As punk exploded on London's fashion scene in the late 1970s, Rhodes produced the Conceptual Chic collection in 1977 that featured edgy evening gowns with slashed skirts safety-pinned to silk bodices and ornamented with ball chains and jeweled studs. In the 1970s and 1980s, Rhodes created gowns for several members of the British royal family, including Princess Diana, who ordered garments from the designer to wear at high-profile events.

Rhodes draws inspiration from many sources, including art and fashion history, ethnic and cultural dress, and theatrical costumes. Her work is known for its exceptional handwork and surface ornamentation that includes appliqué, quilting, and handkerchief hems. She also produced some fabrics to precisely fit the cut or pattern of her garments, known historically by the term "à la disposition." She is involved in the production of ethically sourced fair-trade textiles and fashion in India and Bangladesh that provides employment for local women. —PBR

top right: Zandra Rhodes (British, b. 1940) adjusts model Mie Kringelbach wearing an evening gown from her 1981 Renaissance/Gold collection at the opening of *The Cutting Edge: 50 Years of British Fashion, 1947–1997* exhibition at the Victoria and Albert Museum, London

bottom right and opposite: Zandra Rhodes, evening ensemble from the Conceptual Chic collection, 1977, Kunstmuseum Den Haag, 0242227

JEAN MUIR

Fashion! I hate the word; I hate the overimportance attached to it. I am a dressmaker. It is better used as a verb, not a noun: to fashion, to make, to craft, the art of making, which implies craft and skill.

left: Jean Muir (British, 1928–1995), wedding dress, 1969, Victoria and Albert Museum, Given by Lady Pamela Harlech, T.268-1986

above: Jean Muir, coat, about 1979–80, Kunstmuseum Den Haag, 1001823

ANNE-MARIE BERETTA

above: Anne-Marie Beretta (French, b. 1937), dress, 1981, Kunstmuseum Den Haag, 0634447

left: Anne-Marie Beretta, ensemble, 1984, Kunstmuseum Den Haag, 0242232

HANAE MORI

Before there was Rei Kawakubo (pp. 124–27) or Issey Miyake, there was Hanae Mori. Mori opened her fashion house in 1951 above a noodle restaurant in Tokyo. She started her career to escape the boredom of domesticity and leveraged her talent into a multimillion-dollar international business. Mori began by designing costumes for hundreds of Japanese movies, but it was only after a visit to Paris, where she met Gabrielle Chanel (pp. 38–41), that she became serious about high fashion. Her first ready-to-wear collection, titled East Meets West, debuted in New York in 1965. Not one to adhere to convention, she caused a stir when she designed miniskirts as part of the flight attendant uniforms for Japan Airlines in 1970. In 1976 she opened a salon in Paris, and in 1977 she became the first Asian designer to be appointed a member of the revered La Chambre Syndicale de la Haute Couture. Mori is best known for her elegant evening wear and suits that derive inspiration from the colors, styles, and cut of kimono. —PS

opposite and right: Hanae Mori (Japanese, b. 1926), suit, 1980s, PEM, Gift of Petra Slinkard in memory of Carli Slinkard, 2019.65.1–2

CÉLINE VIPIANA

right: Céline Vipiana (French, 1915–1997), ensemble, about 1975-76,
for Céline, Kunstmuseum Den Haag, 0487524

DONNA KARAN

Design is a constant challenge to balance comfort with luxe, the practical with the desirable.

As an influx of women entered the workforce in the 1980s, Karan set out to prove that "having it all" didn't mean sacrificing dressing well. Her solution: create an uncomplicated system for dressing for a busy world. After ascending the ranks at Anne Klein in her twenties, Karan debuted her first collection under her own name in 1985. Called Seven Easy Pieces, the line consisted of simple, elegant, interchangeable separates that could work in a multitude of professional or casual situations. The precursor to today's "capsule wardrobe," the collection was intended to free the wearer from sartorial decision making to be able to focus on professional goals. Karan's ads, featuring bold imagery of women in politics and leading large corporations, hinted that ambition and elegance went hand-in-hand. In 1988 Karan founded DKNY, a ready-to-wear casual line consisting of straightforward separates meant to last a lifetime. Karan's theory that women would pay for quality and versatility paid off. Although she sold the two companies to move on to new ventures, her name remains synonymous with easy luxury and classic design. —LM

right: Donna Karan (American, b. 1948), body stocking and skirt from the Seven Easy Pieces collection, 1985, PEM, Gift of Alexandra Mahnken, 2019.12.1-2

VIVIENNE WESTWOOD

opposite: Model Kate Moss walks the runway in a tartan wedding dress designed by Vivienne Westwood (British, b. 1941), 1993

left and above: Vivienne Westwood in collaboration with Keith Haring (American, 1958–1990), ensemble, 1983, Kunstmuseum Den Haag, 0550290

I guess I'm a punk because I'm a fighter. You're born with the character you've got, and I will always fight. I can't help it.

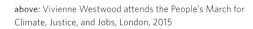

above: Vivienne Westwood attends the People's March for Climate, Justice, and Jobs, London, 2015

right and opposite: Vivienne Westwood, ensembles, 2017

NORMA KAMALI

My interests are people and how they look.

New Yorker Norma Kamali has taken fashion in many new directions and introduced important innovations over the past fifty years. After graduating from the Fashion Institute of Technology, she worked briefly for an airline so that she could travel easily to London and imbibe its fashion atmosphere. In 1968 she and her husband opened a boutique on New York's East Fifty-Eighth Street stocked with styles from London and the base from which Kamali sold her own original designs, ranging from evening gowns to hot pants. After her divorce in 1977, Kamali opened a new firm named OMO Norma Kamali (OMO stood for "On My Own") and expanded her design business.

Launching her career as the women's liberation movement peaked in the 1970s, Kamali captured the mood of women seeking equal opportunity and greater personal freedom by using knits and stretchy fabrics to create "multi-style clothing made for easy care, easy travel." In 1980 she created the Sweats collection, a line of clothing made from sweatshirt fabric that revolutionized sportswear and shifted social norms about casual dress. She created several iconic garments and accessories, such as the "sleeping bag" coat and high-heeled sneakers that were emulated by other designers. Kamali also experimented with more aggressive forms of feminine dress such as body-conscious evening dresses, provocative lingerie, and revealing swimwear—notably the one-piece red swimsuit worn in 1976 by actress Farrah Fawcett in the best-selling poster of all time.

A socially conscious designer, Kamali cites losing friends to AIDS as an impetus to use fashion to promote health and wellness, diversity, and gender-neutral attire. In 2016 Kamali received a Lifetime Achievement Award from the Council of Fashion Designers of America for her contributions to the industry. —PBR

right: Norma Kamali (American, b. 1945), coat, 1980s, Collection of Jimmy Raye, Salem, Massachusetts

opposite: Norma Kamali at home in her signature sleeping bag coat, 2018

ANN DEMEULEMEESTER

I want to be a woman, a man, and a child all together.
I believe in spirit, not in gender.

left: Ann Demeulemeester (Belgian, b. 1959), ensemble, 1989, Kunstmuseum Den Haag,
1007356

above: Ann Demeulemeester, suit, about 1989–90, Kunstmuseum Den Haag, 1007351

MARIELLE BOLIER

right: Marielle Bolier (Dutch, b. 1942), dress, 1992,
Kunstmuseum Den Haag, 1005633

VIVIENNE TAM

There are endless ideas, and you can make the impossible become possible. I want that to be my legacy, trying to make the impossible possible.

Born in Guangzhou, China, Tam grew up in Hong Kong after her family fled China's communist regime. Raised in a sewing family, she picked up the skill early and easily. After completing a degree in fashion design at Hong Kong's Polytechnic University, Tam left for Manhattan in 1982. Working out of a duffel bag, she peddled her first collection door-to-door to the buyers at New York's leading stores. Tam's avant-garde designs utilizing traditional Chinese textiles were a hit, and she soon expanded into outlets in Europe and Africa. After ten years of healthy acceleration, she hit pause. "It's not important how big your business is if the collection isn't right," she said.

After a bit of fine-tuning, Tam reopened in 1992 and showed at New York Fashion Week. Again, her designs struck a chord with an international clientele, but it was Tam's irreverent 1995 collection, featuring Warholian pop images of Chairman Mao by Chinese-born artist Zhang Hongtu, that propelled her into the spotlight. Although controversial, the collection secured Tam her first cover of *Women's Wear Daily*. When the designer finally located a workshop willing to produce the line (many refused), it was shipped to retailers in plain brown paper wrapping. Though Tam recognized the politically charged nature of her collection, her goal was not overtly political; the designer said she wanted to "loosen up Zhang's political art with a bit of fashion." —PS

opposite and right: Vivienne Tam (American, b. China, 1957), "Mao" jacket, 1995–96, Adnan Ege Kutay Collection

BETSEY JOHNSON

above and right: Betsey Johnson (American, b. 1942), ripstop corset dress, 1990s, PEM, Gift of Petra Slinkard in memory of Carli Slinkard, 2019.65.4

opposite: Betsey Johnson fashion show, September 2015

MIUCCIA PRADA

We are still here. We are clever, we are great, we have everything. Why are we not equal?

After an eclectic start that included earning a PhD in political science, training as a mime for five years, and joining the Communist Party, Miuccia Prada reluctantly took over her family's business, Fratelli Prada, in 1978. The luxury leather-goods firm had been founded by her grandfather in Milan in 1913 and produced leather luggage, steamer trunks, purses, and accessories for affluent and aristocratic clients. Prada spent several years learning the business, and in 1985 she launched a line of handbags and backpacks in nylon that were a hit with consumers and soon propelled Prada bags into the lime-light as coveted accessories, and the company into a corporate leader. In 1989 Prada launched her first ready-to-wear collection, which was soon followed by collections noted for streamlined design, precise Italian tailoring and construction, and luxurious materials underpinned by strong conceptual approaches. While some collections tilted toward Minimalism, others suggested whimsical critiques of contemporary culture or musings on historical or cultural dress.

Prada expanded rapidly in subsequent years, launching Miu Miu (Miuccia's nickname) in 1992, a line known for creativity and affordability, and Prada Sport in 1994. Its stores are designed by prize-winning architects such as Rem Koolhaas and Herzog & de Meuron and demonstrate the firm's commitment to architecture and urban design. In 1995 Prada established Fondazione Prada at sites in Milan and Venice, reflecting her interest in contemporary art and commitment to supporting artists, culture, and intellectual pursuits relevant to contemporary life. —PBR

left: Miuccia Prada (Italian, b. 1949), pantsuit, about 1997–98, Kunstmuseum Den Haag, 1029163

MADA VAN GAANS

right: Mada van Gaans (Dutch, b. 1975), ensemble, about 2001, Kunstmuseum Den Haag, 1022809

PHOEBE PHILO

I felt it was time for a more back-to-reality approach to fashion: clothes that are beautiful, strong, and have ideas, but with real life driving them.

A highly accomplished designer best known for bringing functionality and fashion together in unexpected, yet striking ways for the modern, elegant woman, Philo joined Chloé in 1997 as the assistant to Stella McCartney (pp. 134–35). When McCartney left in 2001, Philo stepped into the role of head designer. She helped redefine how twenty-first-century women dressed, focusing on a minimal aesthetic with clean lines and a muted palette. She injected new life into an aging brand and, with it, built a loyal following of fashion insiders. In 2006 she stepped away to focus on family, and two years later accepted the creative directorship at Céline. In 2010 she won British Designer of the Year, and the 2011 International Designer Award from the Council of Fashion Designers of America. When in 2017 Philo stepped down as designer for Céline and Hedi Slimane took her place, the fashion press and her devout followers were devastated. Some grieving the transition launched a "Bring Philo Back" campaign. Needless to say, Philo has left an indelible mark on fashion. —PS

right: Phoebe Philo (British, b. 1973), dress, about 2005–10, for Céline, Kunstmuseum Den Haag, 1056277

opposite: Model in a dress by Phoebe Philo, for Céline, Spring/Summer 2013, Paris, 2012

KATE MULLEAVY / LAURA MULLEAVY

In 2005 Kate and Laura Mulleavy launched their company, Rodarte (their mother's maiden name), from their family's kitchen table. The sisters, home from college, decided it would be fun to channel their love of horror films into fashion, so they cobbled together cash from a waitressing job and the sale of rare records to create a capsule collection of seven dresses and three coats. *Women's Wear Daily* invited the Los Angeles–based duo to its office at the recommendation of Cameron Silver, owner of the LA vintage boutique Decades, and in an unprecedented move, the publication put the unknown sisters' collection on the magazine's front page in February 2005, proclaiming it "starlet chic."

The self-taught pair have been mentored by some of fashion's most formidable players—*Vogue*'s editor in chief Anna Wintour, for one. Within two years of their debut, the Mulleavys were named as Womenswear Designer of the Year by the Council of Fashion Designers of America, the top award in the fashion industry. In 2008 Rodarte produced its most recognized and heralded collection, which included "slasher dresses" inspired by modern Japanese horror films. While Kate and Laura Mulleavy are said to value creative expression over business, they have collaborated with mass-market companies such as the Gap and Target. The sisters also created costume designs for Natalie Portman in the 2010 movie *Black Swan* and directed their first feature film, *Woodshock* (2017), featuring Kirsten Dunst. — PS

opposite: Model in a dress by Kate Mulleavy (American, b. 1979) and Laura Mulleavy (American, b. 1980), for Rodarte, 2009

right: Model in a dress by Kate Mulleavy and Laura Mulleavy, for Rodarte, 2008

ISABEL TOLEDO

My ideal happens to be diversity. I love difference. I love change. I love experimentation and eccentricities.

Fashion designer, seamstress, and sculptor, Toledo created designs derived from a complex examination of organic forms coupled with astute experimentation with cut and cloth. Toledo's clothing was regarded by some in the American fashion industry as peculiar, but the designer carved out a place for herself in high fashion as an experimental genius.

Born Maria Isabel Izquierdos in Cuba, she immigrated to the United States as a teenager in 1968. Soon thereafter she met Ruben Toledo, who became her husband and artistic partner. They married in 1984, the same year she debuted her first collection. Within a year her work was picked up by exclusive avant-garde fashion outlets such as Colette (Paris), Ikram (Chicago), and Joyce (Hong Kong). Toledo shunned the usual rigmarole of the fashion industry. She stopped producing runway shows in 1988, and at the time she designed her most famous work—a two-piece canary yellow ensemble worn by Michelle Obama to the 2009 inaugural parade—she had neither a publicist nor a cell phone. Her work was featured in solo retrospectives at the Fashion Institute of Technology, New York, in 2009 and at the Detroit Institute of Arts in 2018. In 2019 she died of breast cancer at the age of fifty-eight, an unexpected and devastating blow for many in the art and design worlds. —PS

opposite: Isabel Toledo (American, b. Cuba, 1961–2019), "Wave" dress, 2011, Museum of Fine Arts, Boston, Museum purchase with funds donated by the Fashion Council, Museum of Fine Arts, Boston, 2011.2057

CAROLINA HERRERA

I don't get my inspiration from books or a painting. I get it from the women I meet.

Herrera grew up amid wealth and privilege in Venezuela and understood well the world of couture, sometimes even stepping in to help the designers of her own clothes get a fit or look just right. She began her career in fashion in 1965 as a publicist for the Italian designer Emilio Pucci. She appeared on the International Best-Dressed List in 1972 and was elected to its Hall of Fame in 1980. In 1981 she started her own company at the behest of her friend Diana Vreeland, the fashion arbiter and former editor in chief of *Vogue*. Herrera's house specializes in elegant ready-to-wear garments that look, feel, and fit like couture. She has dressed Jacqueline Kennedy, Nancy Reagan, and Michelle Obama and is a favorite of film stars such as Renée Zellweger. Herrera opened her flagship store on New York's Madison Avenue in 2000. In 2008 she was honored with the Geoffrey Beene Lifetime Achievement Award from the Council of Fashion Designers of America. —PS

opposite: Carolina Herrera (American, b. Venezuela, 1939) poses with her designs, New York, 2014

left: Carolina Herrera, dress, 2016, PEM, Gift of Susan Esco Chandler, 2018.34.60

REI KAWAKUBO

I am working on things that don't exist.

Kawakubo is widely recognized as the most visionary, groundbreaking, and nonconformist designer of the past fifty years. After founding Comme des Garçons in 1969, she produced controversial collections and runway shows that upended preconceptions about the relationship of garments to the body, ideals of beauty, and traditional approaches to design and construction. At times Kawakubo's collections evoke monastic simplicity and severity, heightened by the use of black or white as a signature palette. Her use of transparency and layering in traditionally tailored coats and jackets conceal and reveal the body in unexpected and even shocking ways. Kawakubo's bias cuts, pleating, and seaming details recall classic dressmaking, while her deconstructivist approach is highlighted in distressed finishes, unraveling edges, and fragmented or disrupted forms and materials—strategies that intentionally turn designs inside out. Kawakubo mined historical fashion for inspiration while at the same time injecting it with a contemporary edge, as in her Fall 1996 collection, Flowering Clothes, in which velvet garments inspired by Old Master paintings were punked up with safety-pin fasteners. Her Spring–Summer 1997 collection, Body Meets Dress, Dress Meets Body, featured garments with down-filled pads that extend or distort the body and create extreme silhouettes that challenge historical ideals of feminine beauty. Her Fall 2019 collection, A Gathering of Shadows, explored a dystopian vision of the world with sculptural rubber garments inspired by military armaments and politically charged designs that reference global unrest.
—PBR

right: Rei Kawakubo (Japanese, b. 1942), dress, 1970–2014, for Comme des Garçons, PEM, Gift of Lauren Leja, 2014.45.48

opposite: Model in an ensemble by Rei Kawakubo, for Comme des Garçons, 2014

above and opposite: Rei Kawakubo, coat,
1996, for Comme des Garçons, PEM,
Gift of Lauren Leja, 2014.45.52

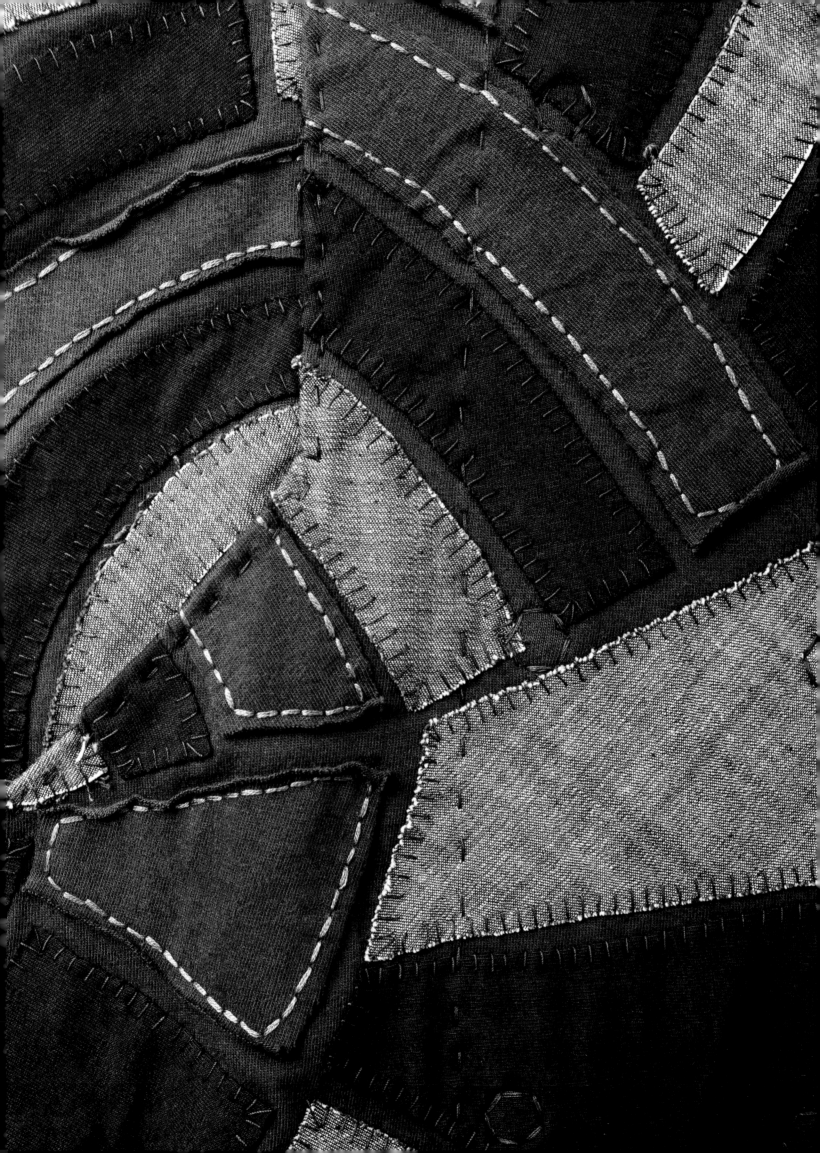

NATALIE CHANIN

The message is not about Alabama. . . . It's about empowering women and rejuvenating local economies, all the while providing an ethically and ecologically clean product.

In 2000, after years as a designer on New York's Seventh Avenue and a stylist and costume designer in Europe, Chanin needed a break and took up sewing. After failing to find manufacturers in New York able replicate the kind of handwork she produced, she decided to return home to Florence, Alabama—once a hub for the cotton T-shirt industry in the United States—because she knew she could find skilled makers there. But since Chanin had left the area in the late 1980s, Florence's garment industry had collapsed. Disheartened yet inspired, Chanin launched Alabama Chanin using discarded T-shirts and employing local seamstresses to create one-of-a-kind handmade garments. The formula worked. She put down roots in Florence and, rather unwittingly, became a pioneer in the sustainable, zero-waste movement. After some critics balked at the expense of her wares, Chanin challenged the industry again, this time by providing step-by-step guides to making her garments. Some thought this gambit was crazy, but it worked: Chanin's clients came to understand the inherent costs involved in the creation of her pieces and, better yet, to respect the process. Chanin has since expanded her business into a multipronged enterprise in which all facets work to create a collaborative community. In 2013 she won the Council of Fashion Designers of America/Lexus Eco-Fashion Challenge, which honors American designers who work in the realm of sustainable fashion. —PS

opposite and bottom right: Model in "Lee" dress by Natalie Chanin (American, b. 1961), 2017, for Alabama Chanin, Collection of Natalie Chanin for Alabama Chanin

top right: Model in "Chandler" jacket and "Austin" skirt by Natalie Chanin, 2018, for Alabama Chanin, Collection of Natalie Chanin for Alabama Chanin

MARIA GRAZIA CHIURI

I have a responsibility to use my position to say something relevant.

The house of Christian Dior was founded in 1947 and is perhaps one of the best-known fashion houses in the world. For seventy years it operated under the direction of men until, in a landmark move, the Italian designer Maria Grazia Chiuri was appointed artistic director in 2016. Prior to her arrival at Dior, Chiuri spent seventeen years at Valentino, eight of which were spent co-leading the brand. During her time there, Chiuri redefined the brand and revitalized it with new energy, producing many iconic designs, such as the Rockstud collection of accessories. The significance of being the first female artistic director of a fashion house known since its founding as the epitome of femininity was not lost on Chiuri. In September 2016 her first collection for the house included the now renowned "We Should All Be Feminists" T-shirt, an item that would make her a design superstar. Chiuri is redefining what it means to be a female fashion designer in the twenty-first century. —PS

opposite: Model in an ensemble by Maria Grazia Chiuri (Italian, b. 1964), for Dior, 2020

right: Model in an ensemble by Maria Grazia Chiuri, for Dior, 2018

MARY-KATE OLSEN
/ ASHLEY OLSEN

What began as a quest for the perfect T-shirt evolved into an internationally renowned fashion house. Conceptualized by child stars-turned-fashion designers Mary-Kate and Ashley Olsen, the brand the Row was launched by the sisters in 2006. The name was inspired by Savile Row, the famed street in London known for its traditional bespoke tailoring for men. It's a fitting appellation for a company catering to a well-heeled, fashion-savvy clientele that includes style icons Catherine "Deeda" Blair and Cate Blanchett interested in exceptionally well-made, streamlined garments created from luxurious fabrics.

The Olsens are not the first actresses to try their hand at fashion, but they are certainly among the most successful. Their honors include the Council of Fashion Designers of America's Womenswear Designer of the Year in 2012 and Accessory Designer of the Year in 2014, and the sisters have successfully extended their reach into secondary markets through collaborations with JCPenney, TOMS, and their own contemporary brand, Elisabeth and James. If the Olsens' endeavor was initially met with skepticism within the industry, over the last decade it has evolved into a well-loved brand. —PS

left: Mary-Kate Olsen (American, b. 1986) and Ashley Olsen (American, b. 1986) of the Row, 2013

STELLA McCARTNEY

I do firmly believe you shouldn't have to sacrifice your style for the sustainability card.

McCartney leads today's fashion community in her commitment to socially conscious practices. In 1997 she became creative director for Chloé, the Paris house known for its luxury ready-to-wear styles, and in 2001 McCartney launched her own label. While her first collection was widely criticized, it featured design elements that evolved into signature styles: classic tailored jackets mixed with lingerie-inspired skirts and blouses, chunky knitwear, and athletic garments printed with slogans. In 2005 she and the athletic-gear giant launched adidas by Stella McCartney, a high-performance sportswear line for women. While she consistently downplays her celebrity parents (Paul and Linda McCartney), McCartney drew inspiration from the Beatles and their 1969 animated film *Yellow Submarine* for her 2019 All Together Now collection, featuring abstract portraits of the four legendary musicians.

From the outset of her career McCartney embraced advocacy and activism for causes including women's rights and health, ethical and sustainable fashion, animal rights, environmental causes, and corporate social responsibility. The McCartney label does not use fur or leather in its fashion lines, and the brand promotes reducing waste, recycling, and eliminating the use of plastics. McCartney's 2017 Spring collection included cheery red-and-white polka dot garments entwined with mottos such as "Thanks Girls," "No Fur," and "No Leather." In 2019 McCartney worked with Google to develop tools to collect and analyze data on the fashion and textile production supply chains of raw materials and their environmental impact. —PBR

top right: Stella McCartney (British, b. 1971). "Thanks Girls" ensemble, 2017

bottom right: Models at the Stella McCartney fashion show, Paris, 2017

opposite: Model in an ensemble by Stella McCartney, Paris, 2017

MARY KATRANTZOU

I understand a woman's body well.

left and above: Models in ensembles by Mary Katrantzou (Greek, b. 1983), 2018

CLARE WAIGHT KELLER

above: Model in an ensemble by Clare Waight Keller (British, b. 1970), for Chloé, 2017

left: Model in an ensemble by Clare Waight Keller, for Chloé, 2015

IRIS VAN HERPEN

I try to sense where "today's" woman is.

Iris van Herpen has stood at the forefront of contemporary, experiential haute couture since the debut of her first collection in 2007. Her innovative and often physics-defying designs worn by models of all ages effectively altered modern thinking about the definition of couture—how it is made and who gets to wear it. Van Herpen achieves her futuristic visions through the successful union of cutting-edge technologies such as 3-D printing and the use of wildly unusual fabrics, metal, and printed plastics. Her pieces are constructed using superb craftsmanship rooted in the couture tradition, while her process capitalizes on her fascination with nature, resulting in designs that manifest as sculpture rather than clothing. Van Herpen continues to break new ground, designing not for the retail market but instead for select clients that include private collectors and museums. Revolutionizing the way the world sees haute couture, and reminding us that it is truly a form of engineering, van Herpen created a style of dress that reflects our present moment by marrying advanced technology with traditional design philosophy. —PS

opposite: Model in an ensemble from the Ludi Naturae collection by Iris van Herpen (Dutch, b. 1984), 2018

above: Model in a dress from the Wilderness Embodied collection by Iris van Herpen, 2013

opposite and above: Models in designs by Iris van Herpen, 2018

KATHLEEN KYE

Making something fun out of serious themes fits my brand quite well.

Kye is a Korean American designer living and working in Seoul. Born in Detroit, she was the youngest student to receive a master of arts degree from Central Saint Martins of the University of the Arts London. There she focused on menswear, which provided her with a strong foundation for her timely unisex streetwear styles. Her Body collection debuted in 2009 and was a huge success. Following appearances on a South Korean television program, Kye launched the KYE brand in 2011 and won the LVMH Prize honoring young designers in 2014, a plaudit followed by the Woolmark award for womenswear for Asia in 2017.

Although she has been on the scene for only a few years, KYE has a robust following that includes K-Pop icon G-Dragon, model Irene Kim, and celebrity Kourtney Kardashian. The designer draws inspiration from the streets, her friends, her love of hip-hop, and her dreams of crafting high-end, high-quality streetwear that is both fresh and covetable. An ardent supporter of Seoul Fashion Week, Kye uses her presentations there as a way to boost emerging Korean models and support the industry in the city she calls home. —PS

right and opposite: Kathleen Kye (South Korean, b. United States, 1987), "Monster" minidress, 2016, PEM, Gift of Petra Slinkard in memory of Carli Slinkard, 2019.65.3

JAMIE OKUMA

Okuma (Luiseño/Shoshone-Bannock) grew up surrounded by artists. Her mother was a Los Angeles–based graphic designer, producing work for performers such as Cher and Lynyrd Skynyrd while working for RCA Records. With her mother's encouragement, Okuma began beading as child. Powwows at Fort Hall Indian Reservation in Idaho inspired her own extravagantly beaded garments for future occasions. At the age of eighteen she enrolled in design classes at Palomar College in San Marcos, California, and briefly attended the Institute of American Indian Arts in Santa Fe. Almost immediately, Okuma began exhibiting her work at Santa Fe's famed Indian Market, where she was the youngest participant ever to win best of show. She still holds this honor and has since won it two more times.

Okuma's reputation is rooted in her intricately detailed and sumptuous beadwork that adorns shoes, handbags, and garments. Living with her community on the La Jolla Indian Reservation, the designer officially launched her own brand in 2015. Her pieces blend modern art and high fashion with time-honored elements in Native culture in a thought-provoking manner and showcase the pride, diversity, and complexity of American Indian women. She is also known for her originality and her fierce pursuit of the next creative challenge. For her 2019 collection the designer sourced sustainable silk and bamboo for use in her clothing. While Okuma is best known for her "indigenized" take on luxury brands, such as Christian Louboutin footwear, she is expanding her reach and style with each passing year. —PS

left: Model in a dress by Jamie Okuma (Luiseño/Shoshone-Bannock, b. 1977), 2018

opposite: Jamie Okuma, glass beads on boots designed by Christian Louboutin, 2013-14, PEM, Museum commission with support from Katrina Carye, John Curuby, Karen Keane and Dan Elias, Cynthia Gardner, Merry Glosband, Steve and Ellen Hoffman, 2014.44.1AB

BECCA McCHAREN-TRAN

It's time to explode our historically narrow view of beauty.

McCharen-Tran is the founder and creative director of the sportswear line Chromat. Since bursting onto the fashion scene in 2010, she and her team have led the conversation in fashion around gender fluidity, racial inequality, and body acceptance. More than a swim- and bodywear company, Chromat is a platform for examining and challenging traditional notions of who is—and what body shapes are—considered "desirable." From its inception the brand made a conscious effort to show its collections on trans and non-gender-conforming models, almost all of whom are people of color with diverse body shapes. The company's #ChromatBABES hashtag on social media serves as a unifying digital battle cry for Chromat fans and the fashion intelligentsia. Even the logistics of the brand's business has pushed the boundaries of what it means to "work in fashion": Chromat moved its headquarters to Miami, sells directly to consumers, and, starting in 2013, produces its line with sustainability and climate change in mind. —PS

opposite: Becca McCharen-Tran (American, b. 1984) with models Ashley Graham and Karlie Kloss in bathing suits by Chromat, 2017

CARLA FERNÁNDEZ

We say death to planned obsolescence, which renders expendable all it draws into its abyss of waste. We believe tradition is not static, and fashion is not ephemeral.

For Fernández, fashion is resistance. At a time of heated conversation around cultural appropriation, Fernández roots her design ethos in honoring the styles, traditions, and cultures of artisans past and present. Born in Saltillo, Mexico, Fernández works out of Mexico City. Her modern conceptualization of garment design proves that ethical fashion can be significant, avant-garde, and forward thinking. Fernández and her team are change agents and advocates for socially conscious business practices, fostering meaningful and respectful partnerships with people in a number of Indigenous communities. In addition to her of line of ready-to-wear clothes inspired by Mexican textiles and patterns, Fernández runs Taller Flora, a mobile design laboratory that works with Mexican designers and local artisans to create couture and ready-to-wear garments. The goal of this endeavor is to show the world how merging traditional and modern aesthetics can push boundaries of fashion. —PS

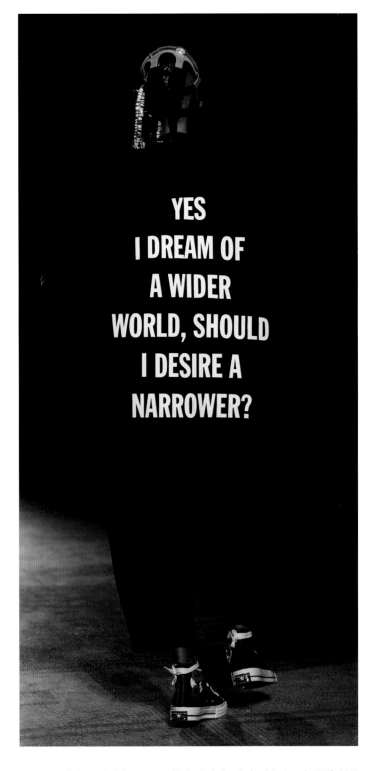

opposite and above: Model in an ensemble by Carla Fernández (Mexican, b. 1973), 2018

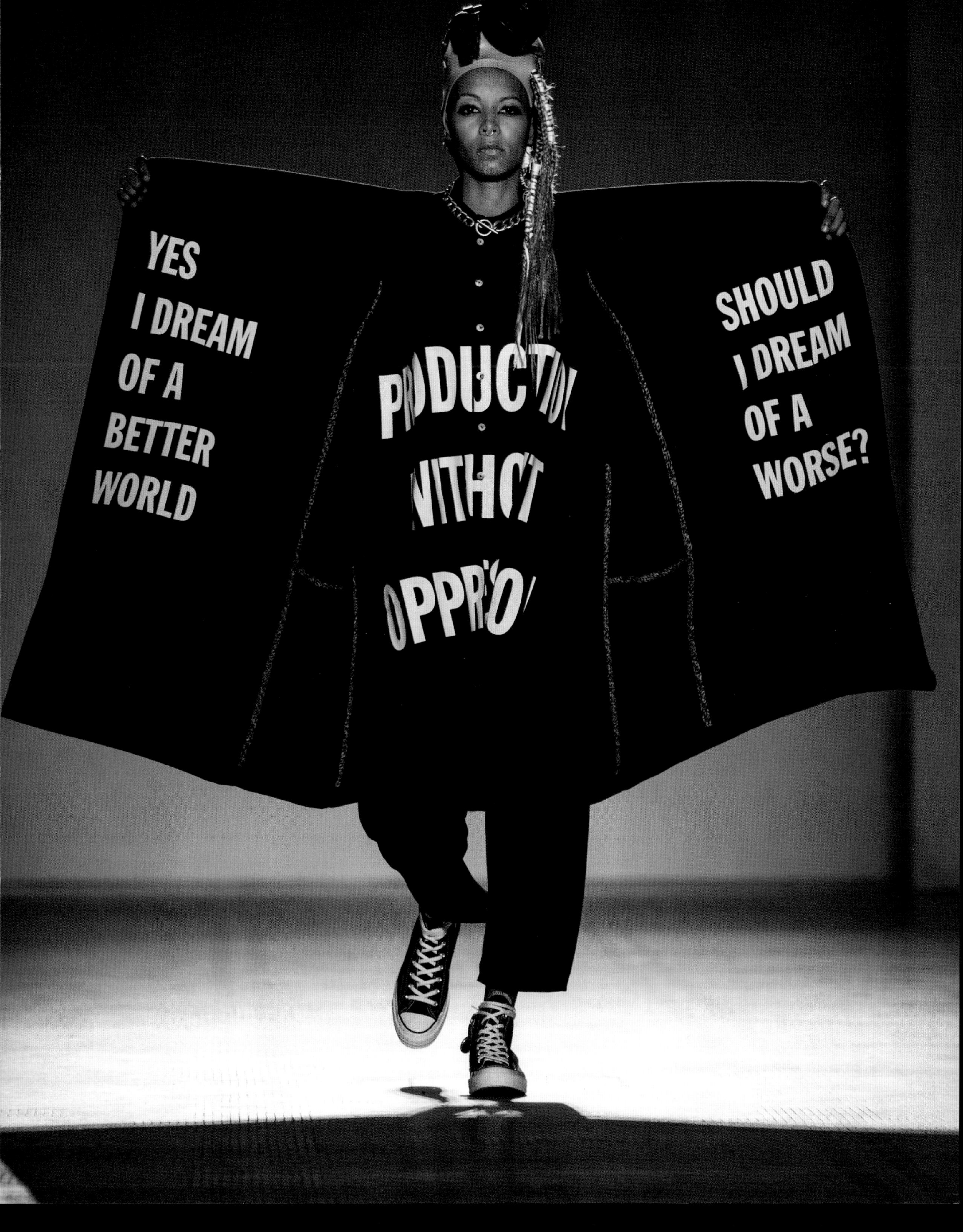
YES
I DREAM
OF A
BETTER
WORLD
SHOULD
I DREAM
OF A
WORSE?

KATHARINE HAMNETT

Fashion is a great tool for putting across political ideas in writing. You can't NOT read messages on T-shirts.

left: British Prime Minister Margaret Thatcher greets Katharine Hamnett (British, b. 1947), who wears her T-shirt with a nuclear missile protest message, at 10 Downing Street, 1984

above: Peaches Geldof and Katharine Hamnett in protest shirts designed by Hamnett, 2007

TRACY REESE

My clothes are not basics, and they're not really classics either, but they are, hopefully, essentials.

Reese, one of a few black female designers to be recognized over time by the fashion industry, is best known for creating clothing that combines unexpected textures, colorways, and materials infused with a vintage feel inspired by music, art, and architecture. Raised in Detroit, she later cut her teeth as an in-house designer with companies such as the Limited, Magaschoni, and Martine Sitbon and then struck out on her own in the 1980s. While her designs have been well regarded, it is only in the last few years that Reese began to use her platform for activism, emphasizing inclusivity and body positivity. Tired of abiding by the accepted rules of the fashion world, Reese kicked off her twentieth anniversary in 2017 with a presentation supporting Planned Parenthood that featured a poetry reading. The show for her Spring 2018 collection, called "The Models Speak," had models of all ages—historically seen and not heard—delivering monologues about themselves, their beliefs, and their dreams while wearing Reese's clothing. In 2018, with the help of Flint, Michigan, residents, the designer collected 90,000 empty water bottles and transformed them into fabric for a capsule collection inspired by the water tragedy in that city. Her new label, Hope for Flowers, begun in 2019, focuses on sustainable materials, ethical production, and slow, purposeful handwork made in Detroit. "I knew it was time for me to look at my career and my dreams and rethink how I was going about the process and ask myself: How can I do better?" — PS

right: Michelle Obama wearing Tracy Reese (American, b. 1964) at the 2012 Democratic National Convention

SELECTED BIBLIOGRAPHY

Aav, Marianne, ed. *Marimekko: Fabrics, Fashion, Architecture.* New Haven, CT, and London: Yale University Press, 2003.

Adichie, Chimamanda Ngozi. "We Should All Be Feminists." Filmed December 2012 in London. TEDxEuston video, 29:21. https://www.ted.com/talks/chimamanda_ngozi_adichie_we_should_all_be_feminists?language=en.

———. *We Should All Be Feminists.* London: Fourth Estate, 2014.

Alford, Holly Price, and Anne Stegemeyer. *Who's Who in Fashion.* 6th ed. New York: Fairchild Books, 2014.

Armstrong, Lisa. "'I Didn't Really Discover Feminism until I Was 48': Dior's Maria Grazia Chiuri on Using Fashion for Political Ends." *Daily Telegraph,* November 29, 2017. https://www.telegraph.co.uk/fashion/people/didnt-really-discover-feminism-48-diors-maria-grazia-chiuri/.

Arnold, Rebecca. *The American Look: Fashion, Sportswear, and the Image of Women in 1930s and 1940s New York.* London and New York: Tauris, 2009.

Bigham, Randy Bryan. *Lucile, Her Life by Design: Sex, Style, and the Fusion of Theatre and Couture.* San Francisco: MacEvie Press Group, 2013.

Bivins, Joy L., and Rosemary K. Adams, eds. *Inspiring Beauty: 50 Years of Ebony Fashion Fair.* Chicago: Chicago History Museum, 2013.

Black, Renata M. "Vivienne Tam—On Staying True to Self." *HuffPost,* December 6, 2017. https://www.huffpost.com/entry/on-staying-true-to-self_b_5106840.

Blum, Dilys E. *Shocking! The Art and Fashion of Elsa Schiaparelli.* Philadelphia: Philadelphia Museum of Art; New Haven, CT, and London: Yale University Press, 2003.

Bolton, Andrew. *Rei Kawakubo/Comme des Garçons: Art of the In-Between.* New York: Metropolitan Museum of Art, 2017.

Borrelli-Persson, Laird. "Rodarte Fall 2008 Ready-To-Wear Fashion Show." *Vogue,* February 4, 2008. https://www.vogue.com/fashion-shows/fall-2008-ready-to-wear/rodarte.

Braun, Sandra Lee. "Forgotten First Lady: The Life, Rise, and Success of Dorothy Shaver, President of Lord & Taylor Department Store, and America's 'First Lady of Retailing.'" PhD diss., University of Alabama, 2013.

Burr, Carole Reid, and Roger K. Petersen. *Rose Marie Reid: An Extraordinary Life Story.* American Fork, UT: Covenant Communications, 1995.

Buttolph, Angela, et al. *The Fashion Book.* London: Phaidon, 2004.

Calahan, April, and Cassidy Zachary. "Global Vision: Tina Leser." Audio recording, 38:26. *Dressed: The History of Fashion* (podcast), September 10, 2019. https://www.dressedpodcast.com/podcasts/global-vision-tina-leser.htm.

Carroll, Berenice. "'Shut Down the Mills!': Women, the Modern Strike, and Revolution." *The Public i* (Urbana-Champaign, IL), March 2012. http://publici.ucimc.org/2012/03/shut-down-the-mills-women-the-modern-strike-and-revolution/.

Carruthers, Claire. "Stella McCartney: 'You Shouldn't Have to Sacrifice Your Style for the Sustainability Card.'" *Vogue Arabia,* January 20, 2019. https://en.vogue.me/fashion/stella-mccartney-on-the-importance-of-sustainability/.

Cartner-Morley, Jess. "Maria Chiuri on Fashion, Feminism, and Dior: 'You Must Fight for Your Ideas.'" *The Fashion, The Guardian* and *The Observer*'s biannual fashion supplement, March 18, 2017. https://www.theguardian.com/fashion/2017/mar/18/maria-grazia-chiuri-fashion-feminism-fight-for-ideas.

Chanin, Natalie. "Natalie Chanin: Bringing Big Fashion to Her Small Town." Interview by Paulette Beete. NEA Arts Magazine (website), 2014, accessed November 21, 2019. https://www.arts.gov/NEARTS/2014v2-story-our-culture-arists-place-community/natalie-chanin.

Charles-Roux, Edmonde. *Chanel and Her World. London,* Paris, and Lausanne: Vendome Press, 1979.

Cole, Daniel James, and Nancy Deihl. *The History of Modern Fashion.* London: King, 2015.

Colón, Ana. "A Decade in, Becca McCharen-Tran Is Still Breaking the Mold with Chromat." *Glamour,* September 5, 2019. https://www.glamour.com/story/becca-mccharen-tran-chromat-10-year-anniversary-interview.

Croft, Claudia. "Miuccia Prada: The Vogue Interview." *British Vogue,* March 18, 2018. https://www.vogue.co.uk/article/miuccia-prada-interview.

Crowston, Clare Haru. *Fabricating Women: The Seamstresses of Old Regime France, 1675–1791.* Durham, NC: Duke University Press, 2001.

Cusumano, Katherine. "Meet Kye, the Up-and-Coming Fashion Designer Who Dresses Everyone from CL to Kourtney Kardashian." *W,* April 2, 2018. https://www.wmagazine.com/story/kathleen-kye-seoul-fashion-designer.

Dague, Sally. "Courageous Spirit Takes Sally Milgrim from East Side New York to Own Salon." *Detroit Free Press,* February 25, 1934. https://www.newspapers.com/image/97663019.

Davis, Nancy, and Amelia Grabowski. "Sewing for Joy: Ann Lowe." Oh Say Can You See? (blog). National Museum of American History, March 12, 2018. https://americanhistory.si.edu/blog/lowe.

Daytona Beach (FL) Morning Journal. "Fashion Designer Ann Lowe Dies." February 28, 1981.

Deihl, Nancy, ed. *The Hidden History of American Fashion: Rediscovering 20th-Century Women Designers.* London: Bloomsbury, 2018.

De Klerk, Amy. "Google Has Teamed Up with Stella McCartney in an Effort to Reduce Fashion's Environmental Footprint." *Harper's Bazaar,* May 15, 2009. https://www.harpersbazaar.com/uk/fashion/fashion-news/a27476402/google-stella-mccartney-environmental-data/.

De la Haye, Amy. *Chanel: Couture and Industry*, London: V&A Publishing, 2011.

De la Haye, Amy, and Shelley Tobin. *Chanel: The Couturiere at Work*, London: Victoria and Albert Museum, 2001.

De Marly, Diana. *The History of Haute Couture, 1850–1950*, London: Batsford, 1990.

———. *Worth: Father of Haute Couture*. London: Holmes & Meier, 1980.

Diderich, Joelle. "Maria Grazia Chiuri Receives Legion of Honor." *Women's Wear Daily,* July 1, 2019. https://wwd.com/fashion-news/fashion-scoops/dior-designer-maria-grazia-chiuri-receives-legion-of-honor-1203210391/ .

Donahue, Wendy. "It's Personal: What Inspires Rodarte's Signature Look? The Mulleavy Sisters' Unique, Laser-sharp Vision." *Chicago Tribune*, May 19, 2013. https://www.newspapers.com/newspage/241545980/.

Drachman, Virginia G. *Enterprising Women: 250 Years of American Business*. Chapel Hill and London: University of North Carolina Press, 2002.

Druckman, Charlotte. "Crafty Cook Natalie Chanin." *Wall Street Journal*, September 7, 2012. https://www.wsj.com/articles/SB10000872396390444914904577623323886048452.

Duff Gordon, Lucy. *Discretions & Indiscretions*. London: Jarrolds Publishers, 1932. https://archive.org/details/in.ernet.dli.2015.208501.

Evans, Caroline, and Minna Thornton. *Women and Fashion: A New Look*. London and New York: Quartet Books, 1989.

Farra, Emily. "'I Need a Few More Colleagues Linking My Arm'—Stella McCartney Sounds Off on Sustainability, Faux Leather, and the Lack of Honesty around Both." *Vogue*, February 15, 2019. https://www.vogue.com/article/stella-mccartney-sustainable-fashion-leather-conversation.

———. "Tracy Reese Unveils a New Sustainable, 'Responsibly Designed' Collection That's Based in Detroit." *Vogue*, June 24, 2019. https://www.vogue.com/article/tracy-reese-new-sustainable-collection-hope-for-flowers-detroit.

Foreman, Katya. "Iris van Herpen Couture Spring 2019." *Women's Wear Daily*, January 21, 2019. https://wwd.com/runway/spring-couture-2019/paris/iris-van-herpen/review/.

Fortini, Amanda. "Twisted Sisters: The Sisters Behind Rodarte." *New Yorker*, January 10, 2010. https://www.newyorker.com/magazine/2010/01/18/twisted-sisters.

Fraser, Kennedy. *Ornament and Silence: Essays on Women's Lives*. New York: Vintage, 1996.

Friedman, Vanessa. "Isabel Toledo Dies at 59; Designed Michelle Obama's Inaugural Outfit." *New York Times*, August 26, 2019. https://www.nytimes.com/2019/08/26/style/isabel-toledo-dead.html.

Fukai, Akiko, et al. *Fashion: The Collection of the Kyoto Costume Institute; A History from the 18th to the 20th Century*. Cologne: Taschen, 2012.

Fürstenberg, Diane von. *The Woman I Wanted to Be*. New York: Simon & Schuster, 2015.

Fury, Alexander. "Is Miuccia Prada the Most Powerful and Influential Designer in Fashion?" *The Independent*, October 6, 2015. https://www.independent.co.uk/life-style/fashion/features/is-miuccia-prada-the-most-powerful-and-influential-designer-in-fashion-a6683801.html.

———. "That's a Wrap, DVF: Diane von Fürstenberg's Dress and the Icon It Has Become." *The Independent*, February 10, 2014. https://www.independent.co.uk/life-style/fashion/features/that-s-a-wrap-dvf-s-dress-and-the-icon-it-has-become-9120145.html.

Gardner, Joan. "Young Designer Weaves Hawaii into New Styles." *Spokane Daily Chronicle*, June 25, 1941.

Golbin, Pamela. *Couture Confessions: Fashion Legends In Their Own Words*. New York: Rizzoli Ex Libris, 2016.

———. *Madeleine Vionnet*. New York: Rizzoli, 2009.

Goldstein, Gabriel M., and Elizabeth H. Greenburg, eds. *A Perfect Fit: The Garment Industry and American Jewry 1860–1960*. New York: Yeshiva University Museum; Lubbock: Texas Tech University Press, 2012.

Hatcher, Jessamyn. "Portfolio: Twenty-One Dresses." *New Yorker*, March 23, 2015. https://www.newyorker.com/magazine/2015/03/23/twenty-one-dresses.

Healy, Claire Marie, "Vivienne Westwood: Youth is Revolting." *Dazed & Confused* 4 (Summer 2018): 128–41.

Hill, Daniel Delis. *As Seen in Vogue: A Century of American Fashion in Advertising*. Lubbock: Texas Tech University Press, 2007.

Hohé, Madelief. *Femmes Fatales: Strong Women in Fashion*. The Hague: Gemeentemuseum; Hasselt, Belgium: Modemuseum, 2018.

Howell, Geraldine. *Wartime Fashion: From Haute Couture to Homemade, 1939–1945*. London: Berg, 2012.

"Introducing Mary Quant." Victoria and Albert Museum, 2019. https://www.vam.ac.uk/articles/introducing-mary-quant.

Jeanne Lanvin. Paris: Palais Galliera, Musée de la mode de la Ville de Paris, 2015.

Kennedy, Alicia, Emily Banis Stoehrer, and Jay Calderin. *Fashion, Design, Referenced: A Visual Guide to the History, Language, and Practice of Fashion*. Beverly, MA: Rockport Publishers, 2013.

Kirke, Betty. *Madeleine Vionnet*. San Francisco: Chronicle Books, 1998.

Koda, Harold, and Andrew Bolton. *Chanel*. New York: Metropolitan Museum of Art, 2005.

———. *Schiaparelli and Prada: Impossible Conversations*. New York: Metropolitan Museum of Art, 2012.

Kramer, Karen, ed. *Native Fashion Now: North American Indian Style*. Salem, MA: Peabody Essex Museum; New York: Delmonico Books–Prestel, 2015.

Kuus, Saskia. "Kinderen op hun mooist: Kinderkleding in de zestiende en zeventiende eeuw" [Children at their best: children's clothing in the sixteenth and seventeenth centuries]. In *Kinderen op hun mooist: Het kinderportret in de Nederlanden, 1500–1700* [Children at their best: children's portraits in the Netherlands, 1500–1700], edited by Jean Baptist Bedaux and Rudi Ekkart. Ghent: Ludion, 2000.

———. "Rokkekinderen in de Nederlanden, 1560–1660: Een onderzoek naar het verschil in kleding tussen meisjes en jongens in rokken" [Childrenswear in the Netherlands, 1560–1660: an investigation into the difference in clothing between girls and boys in skirts]. *Kostuum* (1994): 6–13.

"KYE by Kye Kathleen Hanhee." LVMH Prize (website). Accessed October 7, 2019. http://www.lvmhprize.com/designer/kye/.

Kye, Kathleen. "KYE Language." Interview by Emily Kirkpatrick. *The Wild* (website). Accessed October 7, 2019. https://thewild magazine.com/blog/motion-issue-interview-with-kathleen-kye/.

L. P. Hollander, *Sketches of Boston, 1848–1929*. Boston: L. P. Hollander, 1929.

Lake, Stephanie. *Bonnie Cashin: Chic Is Where You Find It*. New York: Rizzoli, 2016.

Laneri, Raquel. "Why Jackie Kennedy's Wedding Dress Designer Was Fashion's 'Best Kept Secret.'" *New York Post*, October 16, 2016. https://nypost.com/2016/10/16/jackies-wedding-dress-designer-is-finally-recognized/.

Lee, Sarah Tomerlin, ed. *American Fashion: The Life and Lines of Adrian, Mainbocher, McCardell, Norell, Trigère*. New York: Quadrangle/New York Times Book, 1975.

Lubar, Rea. "To Dorothy, Store Biz Was Show Biz." *Daily News* (New York), September 30, 1976. https://www.newspapers.com/newspage/396343351/.

Madsen, Axel. *Chanel: A Woman of Her Own*. New York: Holt, 1990.

Magidson, Phyllis, "Fashion Showdown: New York Versus Paris, 1914–1941." In *Paris–New York: Design Fashion Culture / 1925–1940*, edited by Donald Albrecht. New York: Monacelli Press, 2008.

"Maria Grazia Chiuri." The Business of Fashion (website). Accessed November 13, 2019. https://www.businessoffashion.com/community/people/maria-grazia-chiuri.

Martin, Richard. *American Ingenuity: Sportswear 1930s–1970s*. New York: Metropolitan Museum of Art, 1993.

"Mary Lincoln's Dress" [Elizabeth Keckley]. Smithsonian National Museum of American History (website). Accessed January 25, 2019. https://americanhistory.si.edu/collections/search/object/nmah_515922.

Mead, Rebecca. "Iris van Herpen's Hi-tech Couture: The Designer Combines 3-D Printing and Hand Stitching to Reimagine the Possibilities of the Human Body." *New Yorker*, September 18, 2017. https://www.newyorker.com/magazine/2017/09/25/iris-van-herpens-hi-tech-couture.

Mears, Patricia. *Madame Grès: Sphinx of Fashion*, New Haven, CT: Yale University Press, 2007.

Medeiros, Kimbally A., and Sydonie Benét. "Vivienne Tam." Fashion Encyclopedia (website). Accessed October 8, 2019. http://www.fashionencyclopedia.com/Sp-To/Tam-Vivienne.html.

Mendes, Valerie, and Amy de la Haye. *20th Century Fashion*. London: Thames & Hudson, 2005.

———. *Lucile Ltd.: London, Paris, New York, and Chicago, 1890s–1930s*, London: V&A Publishing, 2009.

Merceron, Dean L., Harold Koda, and Alber Elba. *Lanvin*. New York: Rizzoli, 2007.

Meyerowitz, Joanne J. *Women Adrift: Independent Wage Earners in Chicago, 1880–1930*. Women in Culture and Society. Chicago: University of Chicago Press, 1988.

Milbank, Caroline Rennolds. *Couture: The Great Designers*. New York: Stewart, Tabori & Chang, 1985.

Monsef, Gity, Dennis Nothdruft, and Robert de Niet. *Zandra Rhodes: A Lifelong Love Affair with Textiles*. Edited by Ben Scholten and Madeleine Ginsburg. London: Antique Collectors Club and Zandra Rhodes Publications, 2009.

Morris, Bernadine. "Donna Karan Unveils Clothes for the Everywoman." *New York Times*, September 29, 1988.

Mower, Sarah. "A Scandal Survives: The Story of Fashion Designer (and Titanic passenger) Lucile." *Vogue*, April 13, 2012. https://www.vogue.com/article/a-scandal-survives-the-story-of-fashion-designer-and-titanic-passenger-lucile.

Mulvagh, Jane. "Obituary: Jean Muir." *The Independent*, May 30, 1995. https://www.independent.co.uk/news/people/obituary-jean-muir-1621742.html.

———. "Obituary: Eleanor Lambert." *The Independent*, October 9, 2003. https://www.independent.co.uk/news/obituaries/eleanor-lambert-37241.html

The 1915 Mode as Shown by Paris. San Francisco: Panama-Pacific International Exposition; New York: Condé Nast, 1915. https://archive.org/details/1915mode00pana/page/n3.

Nothdruft, Dennis. "Blurring the Boundaries: Print, Personality and the Interiors of Zandra Rhodes and Christopher Vane Percy." In "Decorative Art and the World of Fashion." Special issue, *Journal of the Decorative Arts Society 1850–the Present*, no. 33 (2009): 26–37. https://www.jstor.org/stable/41809409.

Nothdruft, Dennis, ed. *Zandra Rhodes: Fifty Fabulous Years in Fashion*. New Haven, CT: Yale University Press, 2019.

O'Flaherty, Mark C. "Why We Are Still Crazy about Norma Kamali." *Financial Times*, March 8, 2019.

O'Regan, Kathryn. "Five Things Mary Quant Designed Other Than the Miniskirt." *Sleek Mag*, April 5, 2019. https://www.sleek-mag.com/article/mary-quant/.

Palmer, Alexandra. *Couture and Commerce: The Transatlantic Fashion Trade in the 1950s*. Vancouver: University of British Columbia Press, 2001.

Panhuysen, Bibi. *Maatwerk: kleermakers, naaisters, oudkleerkopers en de gilden (1500–1800)* [Customization: tailors, dressmakers, old-fashioned buyers, and the guilds (1500–1800)]. Amsterdam: Stichting beheer IISG, 2000.

Parkins, Ilya. *Poiret, Dior, and Schiaparelli: Fashion, Femininity and Modernity.* London and New York: Berg, 2012.

Paton, Elizabeth. "A Retrospective Celebrates the Queen of the Miniskirt." *New York Times*, April 4, 2019. https://www.nytimes.com/2019/04/04/fashion/mary-quant-miniskirt-london.html.

Peiss, Kathy. "'Vital Industry' and Women's Ventures Conceptualizing Gender in Twentieth Century Business History." *Business History Review* 72, no. 2 (Summer 1998): 218–41.

Phipps, Betty. "Ann Cone Lowe: A Tampa Legacy Is Honored in New York." *Tampa Tribune*, August 7, 1976. https://www.newspapers.com/newspage/334944174/.

Picardie, Justine, and Karl Lagerfeld. *Chanel: Her Life.* Göttingen: Steidl, 2011.

"Poetry Is 'In' at New York Fashion Week." Poetry Foundation (website). February 13, 2017. https://www.poetryfoundation.org/harriet/2017/02/poetry-is-in-at-new-york-fashion-week.

Polan, Brenda, and Roger Tredre. *The Great Fashion Designers.* Oxford and New York: Berg, 2009.

Pouillard, Véronique. "Design Piracy in the Fashion Industries of Paris and New York in the Interwar Years." *Business History Review* 85, no.2 (Summer 2011): 319–44. https://www.jstor.org/stable/41301394.

Powell, Margaret. "Ann Lowe." Hidden Fashion History (blog). Accessed April 10, 2019. http://hiddenfashionhistory.com/category/ann-lowe/.

———. "The Life and Work of Ann Lowe: Rediscovering 'Society's Best Kept Secret.'" Master's thesis, Smithsonian Associates and the Corcoran College of Art and Design, 2012. https://books.google.com/books/about/The_Life_and_Work_of_Ann_Lowe.html.

Pyper, Jaclyn. "*Style Sportive:* Fashion, Sport, and Modernity in France, 1923–1930." In "Femmes, mode et industrie de la mode dans l'entre-deux guerres (France, Grande-Bretagne, Belgique)." Special issue, *Apparence(s)* 7 (2017). http://journals.openedition.org/apparences/1361.

Quant, Mary. *Quant by Quant.* London: V&A Publishing, 2018.

Reeder, Jan Glier. *High Style: Masterworks from the Brooklyn Museum Costume Collection at the Metropolitan Museum of Art.* New York: Metropolitan Museum of Art, 2010.

Remsen, Nick. "Eco-Fashion Tour de Force Natalie Chanin Has the CFDA in Her Corner." *Elle*, October 30, 2013. https://www.elle.com/fashion/news/a23917/natali-chanin-cfda-lexus/.

Rhodes, Zandra, and Anne Knight. *The Art of Zandra Rhodes.* London: Jonathan Cape, 1984.

Safer, Samantha Erin. "Designing Lucile Ltd.: Couture and the Modern Interior, 1900–1920s." In "Decorative Art and the World of Fashion." Special issue, *Journal of the Decorative Arts Society 1850–the Present*, no. 33 (2009): 38–53. https://www.jstor.org/stable/41809410.

Sapori, Michelle. *Rose Bertin: Ministre des Modes de Marie Antoinette.* Paris: Regard, 2004.

Sargentson, Carolyn. *Merchants and Luxury Markets: The Marchands Merciers of Eighteenth-Century Paris.* London: Victoria and Albert Museum, 1996.

Schiaparelli, Elsa. *Shocking Life.* London: J. M. Dent & Sons, 1954.

Smith, Julia Faye. *Something to Prove: A Biography of Ann Lowe, America's Forgotten Designer.* Create Space Publishing Platform, 2016.

South Florida Sun Sentinel. "Sally Milgrim, Designed and Sold Women's Apparel." June 18, 1994. https://www.newspapers.com/image/239013050/?terms=Sally%2BMilgrim.

Spivack, Emily. "The Story of Elizabeth Keckley, Former-Slave-Turned-Mrs. Lincoln's Dressmaker." *Smithsonian*, April 24, 2013. https://www.smithsonianmag.com/arts-culture/the-story-of-elizabeth-keckley-former-slave-turned-mrs-lincolns-dressmaker-41112782/.

Stanfill, Sonnet, ed. *Italian Style: Fashion since 1945.* London: V&A Publishing, 2014.

Steele, Valerie. *Paris Fashion: A Cultural History.* London, Oxford, and New York: Bloomsbury, 2017.

———. *Women of Fashion: Twentieth-Century Designers.* New York: Rizzoli, 1991.

Strassel, Annemarie. "Designing Women: Feminist Methodologies in American Fashion." In "Fashion." Special issue, *Women's Studies Quarterly* 41, nos. 1–2 (Spring–Summer 2012): 35–39. http://www.jstor.org/stable/23611770.

Sudjic, Deyan. *Rei Kawakubo and Comme des Garçons.* New York: Rizzoli, 1990.

Teunissen, José, ed. *Woman by Vivienne Westwood, Christian Dior Couture, Maison Martin Margiela, Junya Watanabe, Ann Demeulemeester, Veronique Leroy, Bernhard Willhelm, Viktor & Rolf, Hussein Chalayan.* Utrecht: Centraal Museum Utrecht, 2003.

Thomas, Dana. "Iris van Herpen Designs for Nature." *New York Times*, October 1, 2019. https://www.nytimes.com/2019/10/01/style/iris-van-herpen-fashion-netherlands.html.

Tolan, Brenda, and Roger Tredre. *The Great Fashion Designers.* Oxford and New York: Berg, 2009.

Trigère, Pauline. Interview by Paul Green, November 13, 1979. Transcript, Oral History Collection, FIT, The Fashion Industry Leaders. Fashion Institute of Technology, Special Collections and College Archives. https://fitnyc.libguides.com/ld.php?content_id=9520639.

Unruh, Delbert, and Ione C. Unruh. *Forgotten Designers: Costume Designers of American Broadway Revues and Musicals from 1900–1930.* New York, 2018.

Van Godtsenhoven, Karen, Miren Arzalluz, and Kaat Debo, eds. *Fashion Game Changers: Reinventing the 20th-Century Silhouette.* London: Bloomsbury, 2016.

Wagner, Sally Roesch, ed. *The Women's Suffrage Movement.* New York: Penguin Classics, 2019.

Ward, Susan. "'Uniform for Intellectuals': Marimekko, Design Research, and Modernism in Mid-Twentieth-Century Cambridge, Massachusetts." In *Dressing New England: Clothing, Fashion, and Identity: Dublin Seminar for New England Folklife Annual Proceedings 2010.* Edited by Peter Benes. Deerfield, MA: Dublin Seminar for New England Folklife, 2010.

Watson, Linda. *Vogue on Vivienne Westwood.* London: Quadrille, 2013.

Weir, Keziah. "Miuccia Prada: Luxury-Fashion Pioneer." *Vanity Fair*, August 1, 2019. https://www.vanityfair.com/style/2019/07/miuccia-prada-fashion-designer.

Westwood, Vivienne. *Get a Life! The Diaries of Vivienne Westwood, 2010–2016.* London: Serpent's Tail, 2016.

Westwood, Vivienne, and Ian Kelly. *Vivienne Westwood.* London: Picador, 2014.

White, Palmer, and Yves Saint Laurent. *Elsa Schiaparelli: Empress of Paris Fashion.* London: Aurum, 1995.

Wilcox, Claire. *Vivienne Westwood.* London: Victoria and Albert Museum, 2004.

"Woman's Dress, 1911" [Jeanne Lanvin]. Smithsonian National Museum of American History (website). Accessed January 25, 2019. https://americanhistory.si.edu/collections/search/object/nmah_362386.

"Woman's Dress, 1948–58" [Adele Simpson]. Smithsonian National Museum of American History (website). Accessed January 25, 2019. https://americanhistory.si.edu/collections/search/object/nmah_360605.

Wooten, Kristi York. "Alabama Chanin: You Can Make It There." *Bitter Southerner*, January 5, 2016. https://bittersoutherner.com/alabama-chanin#.XcVkfJJKh24.

Yohannan, Kohle. *Valentina: American Couture and the Cult of Celebrity.* New York: Rizzoli, 2009.

Yohannan, Kohle, and Nancy Nolf. *Claire McCardell: Redefining Modernism.* New York and London: Abrams, 1989.

Yotka, Steff. "Maria Grazia Chiuri Makes a Feminist Statement at Her Dior Debut." *Vogue*, September 20, 2016. https://www.vogue.com/article/dior-we-should-all-be-feminists-t-shirt-maria-grazia-chiuri.

Zhang, Tianwei. "Vivienne Tam Goes Big in China: With a Big Show Set for Shanghai, the Chinese-American Designer Shares Her Insights on the Local Market, and Her Personal Journey." *Women's Wear Daily*, March 28, 2019. https://wwd.com/fashion-news/designer-luxury/vivienne-tam-goes-big-in-china-1203093333/.

INDEX OF DESIGNERS AND HOUSES

PHOTO CREDITS

This book is published on the occasion of the exhibition *Made It: The Women Who Revolutionized Fashion* presented by the Peabody Essex Museum, Salem, Massachusetts, on view from May 16 to September 7, 2020. The Kunstmuseum Den Haag organized the original exhibition with curator Madelief Hohé under the title *Femmes Fatales: Strong Women in Fashion.*

Leslie and Angus Littlejohn, Carolyn and Peter S. Lynch and The Lynch Foundation, James B. and Mary Lou Hawkes, Henry and Callie Brauer, Jennifer and Andrew Borggaard, Kate and Ford O'Neil, and Chip and Susan Robie provided generous support. We also recognize the generosity of the East India Marine Associates of the Peabody Essex Museum.

Additional support provided by

 THE COBY FOUNDATION, LTD.   MR·SID

Library of Congress Control Number: 2019952482
ISBN: 9780847868223

First published in the United States of America in 2020 by

Rizzoli Electa, a division of
Rizzoli International Publications, Inc.
300 Park Avenue South, 4th Floor
New York, NY 10010
www.rizzoliusa.com

in association with

Peabody Essex Museum
East India Square
Salem, MA 01970
www.pem.org

Edited by Tom Fredrickson
Designed by Jena Sher Graphic Design
Typeset in Whitney and Champion
Printed in Italy

2020 2021 2022 2023 / 10 9 8 7 6 5 4 3 2 1

Cover: Model in an ensemble from the Ludi Naturae collection by Iris van Herpen (Dutch, b. 1984), 2018, photo by Jean Baptiste Mondino
p. 4: Mada van Gaans (Dutch, b. 1975), ensemble, about 2001, Kunstmuseum Den Haag, 1022809
p. 12: Artists in Europe, gown, about 1740–60, Kunstmuseum Den Haag
p. 20: Sally Milgrim (American, 1891–1944), evening dress, early 1930s, PEM, 133358
p. 28: Maggy Rouff (French, 1896–1971), dress, 1949, Kunstmuseum Den Haag, 0331925
p. 152: Evening dress, about 1920–24, for Callot Soeurs (French, active 1895–1937), Kunstmuseum Den Haag, 322376